Lebanese
Cuisine

Lebanese Cuisine

More than 200 simple, delicious, authentic recipes

Madelain Farah

FOUR WALLS EIGHT WINDOWS

NEW YORK / LONDON

Library of Congress Cataloging-in-Publication Data:

Farah, Madelain.
    Lebanese cuisine/by Madelain Farah.
        p.cm.
    Originally published: Portland, Ore.: M. Farah, 1972.
    Includes index.
    ISBN 1-56858-179-3 (pbk.) 2703 -4775
        1. Cookery, Lebanese. I. Title.
TX725.L434 2001
641.595692–dc21   00-052818

5/02

Printed in Canada

Interior design by Anne Galperin

10 9 8 7 6 5 4 3 2

 TO MY MOTHER

CONTENTS

*If you bake bread with indifference,
you bake a bitter bread
that feeds
but half man's hunger.*

~ KAHLIL GIBRAN

PREFACE

My mother wrote this book as a means to memorialize the recipes of my grandmother. The idea to do so was prompted by a scolding from her father. After moving to Washington D.C. and not having learned to cook, she would call her mother collect, to ask how one dish or another was prepared. After one too many expensive phone bills, her father had had enough. He said, "Either you learn to cook, or you pay for your own phone calls!"

Twenty years later, she set out to write this book. Ingredients were literally captured as my grandmother would throw them into the pot. Recipes were documented, tested, and re-tested so that they would capture the nuances of the old-school cook: "how does it look" or "take a piece and smell for seasonings" or "test for the temperature with your thumb." As a little girl, I watched the entire process, and was an eager taster.

Middle Eastern cooking has become increasingly popular due to its unique flavors, healthfulness, and to the variety of vegetarian dishes. Pita bread, tabbuli and hummus have become so popular that they have lost their association with their originating culture.

This is the how-to for preparation of soul-warming Lebanese foods, which are passed down from generation to generation. Many of us associate joy with the foods of our childhood, many stemming from our ethnic roots. To me, the fondest memories are of my grandmother baking bread. She would make a tiny loaf just for me. I would wait impatiently as it baked, then enjoy it, warm from the oven, dipped in a bit of olive oil. From my mother and grandmother, I learned both the skill and the creative pleasure of home cooking. Today, the most cherished item in my kitchen is an American earthenware bowl that my grandmother used to prepare everything from blueberry pancakes to *laban*.

I hope that you enjoy this book and that it will bring new traditions to your table.

~ *Leila Habib Kirske*

INTRODUCTION

Lebanon . . . the land of the Phoenicians . . . a mosaic of peoples, cultures, mores, and customs; of religions and costumes; crossroads of spice routes and civilizations: all epitomized today in modern Lebanon, a country that still conveys the flavor of the past. This book introduces the art of Lebanese cuisine—recipes that are representative of the Middle East as a whole. While I may be cooking in a modern American kitchen, the aroma of the Lebanese kitchen is the same here as it was for my mother and grandmother in Lebanon.

In the Middle East, not unlike in many other cultures, the chief cook in an extended family is queen of her home, and her throne is essentially in the kitchen. No sooner is breakfast done, than preparation for lunch has begun, and then again for dinner. It takes a measure of oneself in cooking that goes far beyond the measured ingredients. Mealtime in the Middle East is a leisurely and a happy occasion, during which the family is brought together in thanksgiving and mirth.

The time has come, however, when "a pinch of this," or "a little of that," and the "come-and-watch-me" technique of generation upon generation of daughters observing mothers is no longer feasible for the modern mobile family, or for the conscientious cook with limited time to spend in the kitchen. My aim here has been to put down on paper what I learned in the kitchen of my mother. Arabic titles are given along with their English translations. Though there are many local variations for these recipes, with slight changes in ingredients, the names are basically the same.

Colloquial rather than classical Arabic is used in the transliteration of these names. While in most cases the spelling represents sounds that are very similar to those existing in English, the following is a brief description of the symbols, which do not exist in the English alphabet, together with a brief description of the sounds they represent: vowel length and hard consonants are not indicated; ʾ is a glottal stop, which is pronounced like *a* in *ask*; ʿ is a pharyngeal variation of the *a* produced by drawing the tongue as far back into the throat as possible and blowing through the narrow passage in the pharynx; *gh* represents a sound similar to the French *r*; *kh* is pronounced like the *ch* in *Bach*. The foregoing explanation of sounds should help the cook pronounce the names somewhat accurately.

Typically Arabic-speaking people say *ṣaḥtayn* upon completion of a meal. It literally means two healths to you. May you enjoy many happy hours of cooking and *ṣaḥtayn*.

~ Madelain Farah

BREAD AND BREAD DISHES
الخبز واطباق الخبز

ARABIC BREAD:
BASIC BREAD DOUGH
Khubz 'Arabi

SEASONED FLAT TART
Mnaqish biz-Za'tar

ARABIC CHEESE PIZZA
Khubz bij-Jibin

SPINACH TRIANGLE PIES
Sbanikh bil-'Ajin

TRIANGLE MEAT PIES
Ftayir

OPEN FACED PATTIES
Sfiha or Lahm bil-'Ajin

PEPPER PATTIES
Ftayir bil-Flayfli

HOLY BREAD
Qirban

THERE ARE MANY NAMES FOR and forms of Arabic bread: *kmaj, marquq, tlami, saj, furn.* Some are made thick (*tlami*), others, paper thin (*saj*); some are cooked over a metal dome on an open fire, some baked in ovens. However, the basic Arabic Bread recipe is used for all of these variations. It is a trick as well as an art to be able to cook good Arabic Bread. In the Middle East, a woman would set aside one day for making bread and bread dishes, all of which require the basic dough recipe. However, with the conveniences of modern life, bread can be made much more quickly and easily.

HINTS

~ While making the basic Arabic Bread recipe, dip your hands in water when kneading to give a smooth elastic finish to the dough.

~ Where ground lamb is required, ground chuck or ground round may be substituted.

DEFINITIONS OF ARAB BREADS

Kmaj: Round flat bread with a pocket used for sandwiches, dips, Arabic pizzas, and so forth.

Marquq: Very thin, round, flat bread, rolled like Italian pizza dough.

Tlami: Round, flat, soft-textured, thick bread without a pocket used for *mnaqish* and as regular bread.

Saj: Paper thin bread that is baked over a metal dome on an open fire.

Furn: Term used for Arabic bread made commercially.

Arabic Bread: Basic Bread Dough
Khubz 'Arabi

1 package or cake of yeast
1 T. sugar
2 c. lukewarm water
6 c. flour
2 t. salt
⅓ c. milk

Dissolve the yeast and sugar in ½ cup of the warm water. Let stand 5-10 minutes. Place the flour and salt in large bowl making a depression in the center. Combine the remaining water, milk, and dissolved yeast; pour it into the depression. Begin mixing the flour with the liquid making sure all batter on the sides of the bowl is worked into the dough. Knead until a smooth dough results and the sides of the bowl are clean. (Hands are occasionally dipped in more water while kneading to give a smooth, elastic finish.)

Cover the dough with a towel and let rise in a warm place until it doubles in size (2-4 hours). Grab orange-size balls from the edge of the dough and form into smooth balls until all the dough is used. Cover the dough balls with a cotton kitchen towel and let rise on another cloth towel for 30 minutes. Roll the balls into ¼-inch-thick circles. Cover and let rise again on a cloth for 30 minutes.

Heat the oven to 475°. Place the dough directly on racks in the oven. As soon as the dough rises into a mound, 2-5 minutes, place it under the broiler for few seconds until it's lightly browned. Cool.

7-9 LOAVES

NOTE Many of the recipes that follow are made with this basic dough. The dough freezes well.

SEASONED FLAT TART
Mnaqish biz-Za'tar

2 loaves of unbaked Arabic Bread
4 T. *za'tar*
4 T. olive oil
1-2 t. lemon juice, optional, depending on tartness desired

Prepare the Arabic bread dough, and just prior to baking set aside 2 loaves for *mnaqish*. Mix the *za'tar* well with the oil and lemon. Roll the dough into a ½-inch-thick circle. Flute the edges.

Pour the oil and lemon mixture evenly on the dough and smooth it over the surface, pressing it gently with 4 fingers leaving finger impressions on the dough. Place the dough on a lightly greased pizza or cookie sheet. Bake at 475° for about 8 minutes or until golden brown.

2 TARTS

13

NOTE The oil in the mixture may be slightly increased or decreased depending on desired thickness of sauce. *Za'tar* is available in Middle Eastern specialty grocery stores.

ARABIC CHEESE PIZZA
Khubz bij-Jibin

1 individual pita
3 slices of cheese
½ fresh tomato, sliced
¼ t. oregano

Open the pocket of pita from the side leaving half of the circle attached. Arrange the slices of cheese, followed by slices of tomatoes, and top with a sprinkling of oregano. Close the top. Bake at 350° until the cheese is melted.

1 CHEESE PIZZA

NOTE This is perfect for snacks or lunches.

14

SPINACH TRIANGLE PIES
Sbanikh bil-ᶜAjin

FILLING

2 bunches of fresh spinach

1 bunch of green onions

1 medium onion

$\frac{1}{8}$ t. allspice

salt and pepper to taste

$\frac{1}{2}$ c. olive oil

$\frac{3}{4}$ - 1 c. lemon juice

1 pomegranate, shelled, optional

1 c. raisins, optional

1 Arabic Bread recipe (see page 12)

Wash the greens and drain well. Finely chop the spinach, green onions, and onion. To the onions, add the allspice, salt, and pepper and work with your fingers, then mix well with the green onions and spinach, adding the oil and lemon juice. Add either pomegranate or raisins, but not both. If pomegranate is used, reduce the amount of lemon juice to $\frac{1}{2}$ cup.

Working quickly, roll the dough like a piecrust. Cut it into 4-inch rounds. Place a heaping tablespoon of the filling on each round and wrap the dough closed in the shape of a triangle.

Grease the bottom of a baking sheet with oil and place the pies in rows. Bake at 400° until golden brown.

3-4 DOZEN PIES

NOTE When closing the pies, be careful not to get juices on the edges. This will make it difficult to close. If need be, however, dip fingers in flour and close.

TRIANGLE MEAT PIES
Ftayir

FILLING

1 lb. lamb shoulder, coarsely ground

2 medium onions, finely chopped

½ c. pine nuts

⅛ t. cinnamon

salt and pepper to taste

½ Arabic Bread recipe, 3-4 balls of dough (see page 12)

1 lemon, cut into wedges, optional

Thoroughly mix all of the filling ingredients. After the dough has risen for 30 minutes, roll each ball as for a thick piecrust and cut them into 3-4-inch rounds. (Reroll the leftover pieces.) Place a tablespoon of filling on each round and spread it to within ½-inch of the edges. Pinch the edges closed to form a triangle, leaving a small hole in the center in order for the meat to cook. Place the triangles closely together on a well-greased baking sheet.

Bake at 400° for about 20 minutes or until golden brown. These may be served with lemon wedges, which can be squeezed into the center opening of each *ftayir*.

20-25 PIES

NOTE When in a hurry, refrigerated tube biscuits may be used. Just flatten and fill. If the dough seems dry and difficult to seal, lightly dip your fingers in water and seal. *Ftayir* may be frozen.

OPEN FACED PATTIES
Sfiha or Lahm bil-ʿAjin

FILLING

1 lb. lamb shoulder, finely ground
1 large onion, finely chopped
½ c. pine nuts
⅛ t. cinnamon
salt and pepper to taste
1 c. yogurt or 1 T. lemon juice

½ Arabic Bread recipe, 3-4 balls of dough (see page 12)

Thoroughly mix the filling ingredients adding the yogurt or lemon juice last. After the dough has risen, roll each ball as for a piecrust and cut into 3-inch rounds. Flute the edges. Spread a tablespoon of the filling evenly on each individual round.

Place the patties close together on greased baking sheets. Bake at 375° for 20-25 minutes or until golden brown.

2-3 DOZEN

NOTE Yogurt or lemon juice may be omitted from the filling.

Pepper Patties
Ftayir bil-Flayfli

FILLING

1 c. diced red sweet peppers
1 medium onion, grated
½ c. chopped walnuts
½ t. salt
½ t. pepper
juice of half a lemon
½-1 c. olive oil

½ Arabic Bread recipe (see page 12)

Mix all of the filling ingredients. Adjust the olive oil so the mixture is the consistency of a soft meat loaf. After the bread dough has risen, roll it as for a piecrust and cut it into 3-inch rounds. Flute the edge. Evenly spread a heaping teaspoon of the filling on the individual rounds, pressing the filling gently into the dough. Place the patties close together on a greased baking sheet. Bake at 425° for 15 minutes or until the pastry is browned.

2-3 DOZEN

NOTE All of the filling ingredients may be coarsely ground in a food processor. When in a hurry, refrigerated tube biscuits may be used. Just flatten and fill. Green peppers may be substituted for red peppers, or a combination of ¾ cup green peppers and ¼ cup pimento.

HOLY BREAD
Qirban

1 package of yeast
1 T. sugar
1⅓ c. lukewarm water
6 c. flour
½ t. salt
½ t. *mahlab*, finely ground, optional
1 c. milk

Dissolve the yeast and sugar in ⅓ cup of the lukewarm water. Let stand 5-10 minutes. Mix the flour, salt, and *mahlab* in a large bowl, making a depression in the center. Pour the milk, remaining water, and dissolved yeast into the center of the flour. Begin mixing the flour with the liquid until all the flour is well worked into the dough. Knead until a smooth dough results and the sides of the bowl are clean. (Occasionally dip your hands in more water while kneading to give a smooth, elastic finish.)

    Cover the dough with a towel and let it rise in a warm place until it doubles in volume (1-2 hours). Divide into 6 equal parts and form into smooth balls. Cover the dough balls and let rise again on a cloth, about 30 minutes. Roll the balls into ¼- to ½-inch thick circles. After rolling all the balls, press them firmly in the center with a special mold for holy bread, or if you don't have the mold, leave plain. Using a toothpick, prick holes of the 3 points of a triangle just outside the last ring of the mold, spacing the triangles in four equal places around the design. (Be sure the holes do **not** touch the ring.) Cover the dough and let rise 35-40 minutes. Bake at 400° for 15-20 minutes or until golden brown.

    1 LOAF

NOTE When removing the bread from the oven, you could wipe both sides of the loaf with a cloth dipped in rose water. In the Antioch Orthodox religion, 5 loaves are offered to the church. The seal taken from the first loaf becomes Holy Communion; the second, for the Mother of God; the third, for the angels and saints; the fourth, for the living; and the fifth, for the deceased. *Mahlab* is available in Middle Eastern specialty grocery stores.

Bread and Bread Dishes

KISHK SOUP
Shurbat al-Kishk

MEATBALL SOUP
Sherbat al-Qima

MEAT SOUP WITH KIBBI BALLS
Shurbat al-Mawzat maʿ Kibbi

SHANK SOUP
Shurbat al-Mawzat

TOMATO SOUP
Shurbat al-Banadura

KIBBI SOUP
Shurbat al-Kibbi

SOUPS
الشوربة

VEGETABLE SOUP
Shurbat al-Khudar

LENTILS WITH
SWISS CHARD
'Adas bis-Silq

LENTIL SOUP WITH OIL
Shurbat al-'Adas biz-Zayt

LENTILS WITH DRIED
BEANS AND RICE
Makhluta

LENTILS WITH ARABIC
STYLE NOODLES
Rishta

SOUP IS A POPULAR DISH that is made from a variety of cereals and vegetables. A favorite winter soup is made from *kishk*, which is yogurt and *burghul* fermented together, dried, and ground. Most Arabic soups are hearty dishes and may be used as the main course.

In Lebanon *kishk* is made by individual families once a year during the summer. The yogurt and *burghul* are put in the sun to dry. A favorite place is rooftops that are flat and clean. When it is time to grind the dried yogurt and *burghul* into *kishk,* relatives will help each other in completing this project. This is a time for mixing merriment with work!

HINTS

~ *Zafra* are the foamy curds resulting from the boiling of meat in water. Remove by skimming as it forms.

~ A cinnamon stick is always added to the water for extra flavoring.

~ When using parsley, add during the last 5 minutes to retain its flavor and color.

~ *Kishk* is available in Middle Eastern specialty grocery stores.

KISHK SOUP
Shurbat al-Kishk

½ lb. lamb, finely diced
1 small potato, peeled and finely chopped, optional
1 large onion, coarsely chopped
3-4 large cloves garlic, coarsely chopped
1 c. *kishk*
4-5 c. water
⅛ t. pepper
salt to taste

Sauté the lamb and potato in a saucepan for a few minutes. Add the onions and garlic and continue sautéing. Add the *kishk* and continue sautéing for a few minutes. Stir constantly after the *kishk* has been added to prevent lumping and scorching. Gradually add the water until a smooth mixture is formed. Cook for about 20 minutes or until thickened (consistency of cream gravy), stirring occasionally.

8 SERVINGS

NOTE *Kishk* is usually salty, so adjust accordingly. The meat may be omitted if desired. *Kishk* is often served during the winter months.

Meatball Soup
Shurbat al-Qima

1 small onion, minced
salt and pepper to taste
½ lb. ground beef or lamb
½ c. parsley, finely chopped
1 t. butter
6-8 c. cold water
1 cinnamon stick
½ c. uncooked rice
1 ripe tomato, diced, optional
salt to taste
powdered cinnamon to taste

24

Mix the onions with the salt and pepper. Add the meat and a few leaves of chopped parsley. Mix well. Make meatballs (or *kafta*) the size of a walnut. Brown the meatballs in the butter. Add a small amount of water (½ cup) to the skillet to deglaze the residue. Empty the meatballs and the stock into a saucepan and add the cinnamon stick and the remaining water. Let it boil on medium heat for 10 minutes, then add the rice, tomatoes, and additional salt to taste. Cook for about 30 minutes or until the rice is tender.

Add the remaining chopped parsley during the last 5 minutes of cooking time. Serve the soup with a dash of cinnamon on top.

8 SERVINGS

NOTE Parsley should not be overcooked in soup, otherwise the flavor is lost.

Meat Soup
with Kibbi Balls
Shurbat al-Mawzat ma' Kibbi

2-3 lamb or 1-2 beef shanks
1 small onion, chopped
$\frac{1}{8}$ t. cinnamon
salt and pepper to taste
7-8 c. cold water
$\frac{1}{4}$ c. uncooked rice

$\frac{1}{2}$ Basic *Kibbi* recipe (see page 102)

Place the meat shanks, onions, seasonings, and cold water in a pot. Cover and cook until a fork can pierce the meat, approximately 1 hour. Add the rice and continue cooking until done, about 30 minutes more.

In the meantime, take the *kibbi* and form it into about 3 dozen walnut-sized balls. These balls may be fried, baked, or broiled until just short of being done. When the shank meat is done, debone it, and return the meat to the broth with the rice. Add the *kibbi* balls and continue simmering for 15 minutes. Add more water as needed.

8 SERVINGS

SHANK SOUP

Shurbat al-Mawzat

3-4 lamb or 2-3 beef shanks
1 cinnamon stick
½ c. uncooked long grain rice
2 tomatoes, diced
salt to taste
⅔ c. parsley, coarsely chopped
powdered cinnamon

Place the lamb or beef shanks and the cinnamon stick in a large Dutch oven and completely cover with cold water. Cover and cook until a fork can pierce the meat, approximately 1 hour. Remove the *zafra*, or fat curds, during the cooking process. Add the rice, tomatoes, and salt and cook until the rice is tender. In the last 5 minutes, add the parsley. To serve, sprinkle with a dash of cinnamon.

8 SERVINGS

Tomato Soup

Shurbat al-Banadura

1-2 beef or lamb shanks
1 cinnamon stick
½ c. uncooked long grain rice
1 lb. well-ripened tomatoes, squeezed and strained
salt and pepper to taste

Place the shanks and cinnamon stick in a large Dutch oven with water just to cover. Cover and cook until tender, about 1 hour. Remove the *zafra*, or fat curds, as it accumulates. Add the rice and cook for 20 minutes. Add the tomatoes, salt and pepper. Simmer for 15-20 minutes.

8 SERVINGS

27

KIBBI SOUP
Shurbat al-Kibbi

½ Basic *Kibbi* recipe (see page 102)

¼ c. pine nuts
1 t. butter
1 onion, minced
7-8 c. water
1 cinnamon stick
salt and pepper to taste
½ c. uncooked long grain rice
½ c. parsley, coarsely chopped

Form the *kibbi* into walnut-sized balls. Make a hole in the center of each ball, place a few pine nuts inside, and close. Brown the *kibbi* balls in the butter. Remove and set aside. Sauté onions lightly. Add a small amount of water to the butter drippings. Pour the drippings into a large pan; add the remaining water, seasonings, and rice. Cook for 20 minutes.

Add the *kibbi* balls and simmer for 20 minutes or until the *kibbi* and rice are done. In the last 5 minutes, add the chopped parsley.

8 SERVINGS

VEGETABLE SOUP
Shurbat al-Khudar

1-2 beef or lamb shanks
6-8 c. water
1 cinnamon stick
1 stalk celery
2 carrots
1 small onion
1 parsnip
1 turnip
4-5 fresh string beans
2 medium tomatoes
1 medium potato
salt and pepper to taste
3-4 stems of parsley, chopped
cinnamon to taste

Place the shanks and cinnamon stick in a pan with the water. Cover and cook until tender, about 30 minutes. Remove the *zafra*, or fat curds, as they accumulate. Dice all the vegetables, except the parsley, in 1-inch cubes and add with the seasonings to the shanks. Cook until the vegetables are tender, about 20 minutes. Add the chopped parsley in the last 5 minutes of cooking. The soup is served with a dash of cinnamon.

8 SERVINGS

Lentils with Swiss Chard
ʿAda̧s bis-Silq

1 c. dried lentils
6 cups water
1 large potato, diced
½ bunch of Swiss chard, coarsely chopped
1 medium onion, coarsely chopped
salt and pepper to taste
3 T. olive oil
lemon wedges

Wash the lentils. Put the lentils and the water in a pot, cover and cook until almost tender, about 30-45 minutes. Add the potatoes; boil for 10 minutes. Add the Swiss chard. Meanwhile sauté the onions with salt and pepper in the oil until the onions are golden brown. Add the onions to the lentil mixture and cook until all of the vegetables are done, no more than 10 minutes. Serve with lemon wedges.

6 SERVINGS

LENTIL SOUP WITH OIL

Shurbat al-ʿAdas biz-Zayt

1 c. split or whole dried lentils
7-8 c. water
¼ c. uncooked rice
1 large onion, coarsely chopped
½ c. olive oil
salt and pepper to taste

Rinse and drain the lentils. Place them in a pot with the water. Cook for 15 minutes. Add the rice. Sauté the onions in the oil. Add salt and pepper. Add the onion mixture to the lentils and rice shortly after adding the rice. Cook for 20 minutes or until tender.

8 SERVINGS

NOTE There are 2 good variations of this recipe. *Shurbat al-ʿAdas maʿ Lahmi* (Lentil Soup with Meat), which you prepare by adding a cup of chopped lamb to the onions, or *Shurbat al-ʿAdas bis-Samni* (Buttered Lentil Soup), which is prepared with butter instead of oil for the sautéing.

LENTILS WITH DRIED BEANS AND RICE

Makhluta

¼ c. dried lentils
¼ c. dried garbanzo beans
¼ c. dried lima beans
¼ c. dried black beans
7-8 c. water
1 T. cumin
1 large onion, coarsely chopped
½ c. olive oil
¼ c. rice
salt to taste

Wash all the dried beans and soak them overnight. Drain. Place the beans in a pot with the water and cover. Bring to a boil, add the cumin, reduce the heat, and cook on medium heat. Meanwhile, sauté the onion in the oil. After the beans have cooked on medium heat for 30 minutes, add the rice, onions, and salt. Cook until all of the ingredients are tender, about 20 minutes more.

6 SERVINGS

NOTE This is an appropriate dish for the Lenten season. The consistency is similar to chili, however, it may be thinned according to personal taste.

LENTILS WITH ARABIC STYLE NOODLES

Rishta

1 ball Arabic Bread dough (see page 12)

1 c. dried lentils
7-8 c. water
1 large onion, coarsely chopped
1 T. olive oil
1 clove garlic
1 T. sweet basil
1 T. coriander seed
salt and pepper to taste
4 c. Swiss chard, coarsely chopped
lemon wedges

Roll the dough like a piecrust and cut it into ¼-inch strips. Then slice the dough diagonally into ¼- to 1-inch-length pieces.

Rinse the lentils. Place the lentils and the water in a pot. Cook until almost tender, 30-45 minutes. Sauté the onions in the oil. Mash together the garlic, basil, coriander, and salt and pepper. Add this mixture to the onions and continue sautéing until the onions are limp. Add this mixture, the Swiss chard, and the dough pieces to the lentils. Cook until the Swiss chard and dough are tender, about 15 minutes. Serve with lemon wedges.

4-6 SERVINGS

SALADS
السلطات

ARABIC SALAD SUPREME
Tabbuli

TOMATO SALAD
Slatat al-Banadura

LEBANESE BREAD SALAD
Fattush

VEGETABLE SALAD
Slatat al-Khudar

PURSLANE SALAD
Slatat al-Farfhin (or Baqli)

SPINACH SALAD
Slatat as-Sbanikh

CAULIFLOWER WITH TARATUR
Qarnabit bit-Tahini

GREEN BEAN SALAD
Lubyi Mtabbli

**GREEN BEANS
WITH POTATO SALAD**
Batata Mtabbli Ma' Lubyi

LEBANESE POTATO SALAD
Batata Mtabbli

**POTATOES WITH
TARATUR SAUCE**
Batata bit-Tahini

BLACK-EYED PEA SALAD
Lubyi Msallat

EGGPLANT SALAD
Batinjan Mtabbal

LIMA BEAN SALAD
Fasulya biz-Zayt

BRAIN APPETIZER
Nkha'at Mtabbli

LAMB TONGUE SALAD
Lsanat Mtabbli

IN THE MIDDLE EAST, most homes have a plentiful variety of vegetables in their gardens. In many parts of the United States there is also a wide selection, including some that are considered weeds—such as purslane and dandelions.

    The basic dressing for all salads is olive oil, lemon juice, and garlic. Olive oil is used in the Middle East, primarily because it is so plentiful. Vegetable oils may be substituted, but there will be slight differences in flavor. Fresh lemon juice is preferable, but concentrated lemon juice may be substituted. Tartness is adjusted according to individual tastes.

ARABIC SALAD SUPREME
Tabbuli

¾ c. *burghul* (crushed wheat, #2)
2 large bunches of parsley, approximately 4 c. when finely chopped
1 c. finely chopped fresh mint or ¼-⅓ c. dried mint
½ bunch of green onions, with green ends, finely chopped
⅛ t. cinnamon
2-3 t. salt
pepper to taste
1 small onion, finely chopped
1 or 2 large tomatoes, finely chopped
½-⅔ c. fresh lemon juice
½ c. olive oil
grape leaves, Romaine, or leaf lettuce

Rinse the *burghul*, drain, then squeeze the excess water out. Place the burghul in a large mixing bowl. Place the parsley, mint, and green onions in layers on top of the *burghul* in the order given. Add the seasonings to the onions and mix thoroughly. Put onions on half of the top layer and tomatoes on the other half. Add lemon juice and toss the salad with a spoon and fork. Just before serving, add the oil and toss thoroughly. Serve with grape leaves or lettuce on the side.

6 SERVINGS

NOTE This is typically eaten by hand. Use the grape leaves, Romaine lettuce, or head lettuce to pick up *tabbuli* in bite-size servings. *Tabbuli* may be prepared 1-2 hours ahead of time by omitting the tomatoes and oil. Just cover with plastic wrap and refrigerate. Add the tomatoes and oil just before serving.

Tomato Salad
Slatat al-Banaдura

1 small clove garlic
¼ t. salt
¼ c. lemon juice
2 cucumbers
3 tomatoes
1 small onion, chopped
¼ c. olive oil

Mash the garlic and salt in a bowl. Add the lemon juice and mix well. Cut the cucumbers and tomatoes into bite-size pieces. Add both to the garlic mixture along with the onions and oil. Mix gently.

6 SERVINGS

38

NOTE This is especially good with sides of hot peppers, olives, and Arabic Bread (see page 12).

LEBANESE BREAD SALAD
Fattush

½ loaf of Arabic Bread (see page 12)

1 small clove garlic

salt and pepper to taste

½ c. lemon juice

½ c. parsley

3 green onions

1 c. fresh mint or ¼ c. dried mint

4-5 large leaves of Romaine lettuce, or ¼ head of lettuce

1 cucumber, peeled, quartered, and cut into small pieces

2-3 medium tomatoes, cut into 1-inch cubes

1 small hot pepper, minced, optional

½ t. *simmaq*, if available

½ c. olive oil

Toast the bread to a golden brown and break it into 1 ½-inch pieces. Set aside.

In a salad bowl, mash the garlic, or use a garlic press, and mix the garlic well with the salt and pepper. Add the lemon juice to the garlic mixture and blend well. Coarsely chop the parsley, green onions, and mint. Tear the lettuce as for a tossed green salad. Add the parsley, green onions, mint, cucumber, tomatoes, hot pepper, simmaq, and toasted bread to the lemon and garlic mixture and toss thoroughly. Just before serving, add the oil and toss well.

6 SERVINGS

NOTE *Simmaq* is available in Middle Eastern specialty grocery stores.

VEGETABLE SALAD
Slatat al-Khuдar

1 clove garlic
¼ t. salt
½ small hot pepper, optional
¼ c. lemon juice
several stems of parsley, coarsely chopped
several stems of mint, coarsely chopped
1 small onion, finely chopped
2 green onions, coarsely chopped
1 small green pepper
4 leaves Romaine lettuce, or other lettuce
1 medium cucumber
2 medium tomatoes
¼ c. olive oil

Mash the garlic, salt, and hot pepper together. Add the lemon juice and mix well. Combine the parsley, mint, onion, and green onion. Set aside. Cut all of the vegetables into chunks and add them to the garlic mixture. Add the parsley mixture and oil to the vegetables and garlic. Toss thoroughly.

4 SERVINGS

NOTE Any combination of vegetables may be used, depending upon what is available.

Purslane Salad
Slatat al-Farfhin (or Baqli)

4 bunches of purslane
1 clove garlic
1 t. salt
¼ c. lemon juice
1 onion, chopped
¼ c. olive oil
1 tomato, chopped
1 cucumber, chopped

Pick or remove the tender, green leaves and clusters at the end of the purslane stems. Discard the seed in the center of the clusters. Wash and drain.

Mash the garlic and salt together. Add the lemon juice and mix well. Add the purslane, onion, and olive oil. Add the tomato and cucumber. Toss lightly.

4 SERVINGS

NOTE Purslane is not typically available in grocery stores. It grows wild in yards and other places, especially around tomato or rose plants. It is considered a weed, but makes an unusual and delicious salad. Pick it in the early morning or late afternoon, so the leaves will be crisp.

SPINACH SALAD
Slatat as-Sbanikh

1 bunch of spinach
1 small clove garlic
1 t. salt
¼ c. lemon juice
½ bunch of green onions, chopped
¼ c. olive oil

Rinse the spinach well and drain thoroughly. Mash the garlic and salt together. Add the lemon juice and mix well. Coarsely chop the spinach and add it with the onions to the lemon juice mixture. Add the oil and toss. Serve immediately.

4 SERVINGS

42

CAULIFLOWER WITH TARATUR
Qarnabit bit-Tahini

1 small head cauliflower, approximately 1 lb.
1 clove garlic
1 t. salt
3 T. *tahini*
2 T. water or cauliflower liquid
⅓ c. lemon juice

Rinse the cauliflower and break it into separate florets. Cook for 15 minutes on a medium flame. When done, the cauliflower should be tender but firm.

Mash the garlic and salt in a bowl. Add the *tahini* and blend well, then add the water and mix thoroughly. Add the lemon juice and blend until the sauce is whitish and smooth. Drain the cauliflower and place it in a shallow bowl. Carefully pour the *tahini* sauce over all of the cauliflower pieces—do not stir. Serve hot or cold.

4 SERVINGS

43

GREEN BEAN SALAD
Lubyi Mtabbli

1½ lbs. green beans
1 small clove garlic
1 t. salt
⅓ c. lemon juice
1 small onion, chopped
2-3 stems parsley, coarsely chopped
⅓ c. olive oil

Wash the green beans, then snip the ends and cut into 2-inch pieces. Cook in salted water until tender but crisp, approximately 3-5 minutes. Drain and cool. Mash the garlic and salt together. Add the lemon juice and mix well. Add the remaining ingredients and toss.

4-6 SERVINGS

44

GREEN BEANS WITH POTATO SALAD
Batata Mtabbli Ma⟨ Lubyi

½ lb. green beans
3 medium potatoes
1 small clove garlic
1 t. salt
⅓ c. lemon juice
1 small onion, chopped
⅓ c. olive oil

Wash the green beans, then snip the ends, and cut into 2-inch pieces. Cook the beans in salted water until tender but crisp, approximately 3-5 minutes. Drain and cool. Boil the potatoes. Cool and cut into 1-inch cubes. Mash the garlic and salt together. Add the lemon juice and mix well. Add the potatoes, beans, onions, and oil. Toss well.

4-6 SERVINGS

NOTE This recipe may be prepared ahead of time for a thorough blending of flavors.

45

LEBANESE POTATO SALAD
Batata Mtabbli

4 large potatoes
1 small clove garlic
1 t. salt
1 t. pepper
⅓ c. lemon juice
1 small onion, chopped
⅓-½ c. coarsely chopped parsley
⅓ c. olive oil

Boil the potatoes. Cool and cut into 1-inch cubes. Mash the garlic with the seasonings. Add the lemon juice and stir well. Add the rest of the ingredients and toss, mixing well.

4-6 SERVINGS

46

POTATOES WITH TARATUR SAUCE
Batat bit-Tahini

4 medium potatoes
1 small clove garlic
1 t. salt
4 T. *tahini*
2 T. water
⅓ c. lemon juice
4 stems parsley, finely chopped

Boil the potatoes until tender, but firm, for about 15 minutes. Cut into ½-inch cubes and place in a bowl.

Mash the garlic and salt together in a small bowl. Add the *tahini* and blend well. Add the water and mix thoroughly. Add the lemon juice and blend until the sauce is whitish. Mix in the parsley. Pour the *tahini* mixture over the potatoes and mix gently so as not to mash the potatoes. This may be served warm or cold.

4 SERVINGS

NOTE This is especially good with baked or fried fish.

BLACK-EYED PEA SALAD
Lubyi Msallat

1 c. dried black-eyed peas
1 clove garlic
1 t. salt
¼ c. lemon juice
1 small onion, finely chopped
½ c. parsley, chopped
¼ c. olive oil

Wash the beans well and soak them in water overnight. Drain and place in a saucepan with water to cover. Cook on a medium flame until tender, but firm. (Check occasionally and add water to cover if needed.)

Mash the garlic and salt together in a large bowl. Add the lemon juice and onions. Drain the beans, reserving one cup of liquid. Add the liquid to the lemon juice mixture. Add the drained beans. Mix well, being careful not to mash the beans. Garnish with chopped parsley in a ring in the center. Pour oil on top. Serve hot or cold.

4-6 SERVINGS

NOTE Two 8-oz. packages of frozen black-eyed peas may be used. Follow the directions on the package and proceed as above.

EGGPLANT SALAD
Batinjan Mtabbal

1 large eggplant
1 small clove garlic
1 t. salt
$\frac{1}{3}$ c. lemon juice
1 T. olive oil
4 stems parsley, finely chopped

Place the eggplant on a baking sheet and bake at 350° until tender but firm. Peel and slice it in large pieces (about 2-inch pieces). Place the eggplant in a large bowl.

Mash the garlic and salt together. Add the lemon juice and blend well. Stir in the oil and pour the mixture over the top of the eggplant. Garnish with parsley. Serve warm or cold.

4-6 SERVINGS

49

NOTE The eggplant may be cubed instead of sliced and tossed with a few chopped pieces of parsley.

LIMA BEAN SALAD
Fasulya biz-Zayt

1 c. dried white lima beans
1 clove garlic
1 t. salt
¼ c. lemon juice
¼ c. olive oil
½ c. finely chopped parsley
3 scallions, chopped, optional

Wash the beans thoroughly and soak them in water overnight. Drain the beans, then place them in a saucepan and cover with fresh water. Cook until tender but firm, about 1½-2 hours. (Check the water and add more to cover if needed.) Drain the beans, reserving ½ cup of liquid.

In a bowl, mash the garlic and salt together. Add the lemon juice and mix well. Add the reserved bean liquid and olive oil to the lemon juice mixture. Add the beans. Toss gently.

Garnish with parsley and scallions, which are sprinkled in a ring on top and in the center. Serve hot or cold, as a salad or a side dish.

4-6 SERVINGS

BRAIN APPETIZER
Nkhaʿat Mtabbli

1 lb. lamb or beef brains
1 t. salt, plus 1 t.
1 clove garlic
2 t. pepper
juice of one lemon, adjust to desired tartness
¼ c. olive oil
½ c. chopped parsley

Rinse the brains and place them in pan of water to cover. Add one teaspoon of the salt. Cook for 10-15 minutes on medium flame or until tender—when the fork pierces the meat easily. Remove the brains and peel off the skin and blood vessels. Cool. Cut the brains in bite-size pieces and place in shallow bowl.

Meanwhile, mash the garlic, remaining salt, and pepper together. Add the lemon juice and oil and mix well. Pour the mixture over the brains, covering all pieces. Sprinkle the parsley on top. Do not stir.

4 SERVINGS

LAMB TONGUE SALAD
Lʃanat Mtabbli

6 lamb tongues
1 clove garlic
2 t. salt, plus 1 t.
2 t. pepper
⅓ c. lemon juice
¼ c. olive oil
½ c. chopped parsley

Rinse the lamb tongues well and place them in a pan. Cover with water and add 2 teaspoons of salt. Cook until well done—when the fork pierces the meat easily. Remove the tongues, cool slightly, and peel off the skin. Cut into 1-inch squares.

Mash the garlic, remaining salt, and pepper together. Add the lemon juice and olive oil, and blend well. Add the tongue pieces to the lemon mixture. Toss. Garnish with parsley.

6 SERVINGS

NOTE This is good as a main course or an appetizer. Another option would be to pour Parsley in Tahini Sauce (see page 188) over the tongue.

FISH
الاسماك

SNAILS
Bizzaq

HERRING HORS D'OEUVRES
Sanamura

GRILLED FISH
Samak Mishwi

FISH WITH PINE NUT SAUCE
Samak Ma⁽ at-Taratur

FISH WITH RICE
Sayyadiyyi

MARINATED FISH FILLETS
Filetto as-Samak

BAKED FISH SUPREME
Tajin

**BAKED FISH
WITH TAHINI SAUCE**
Samak bit-Taratur

**SAVORY SALMON
WITH SPINACH**
Samak bis-Sbanikh

ONE FAVORITE FISH IN LEBANON is called *bizri*, a small, thin fish that is deep fried and eaten like French fries. Other favorites are called *hanklis* and *sultan Ibrahim* and are not generally found in North America. However, ling cod, king fish, bass, and perch can be substituted. After frying fish, one custom is to fry pieces of Arabic Bread in the fish residue to be served as an accompaniment.

SNAILS
Bizzaq

2 dozen fresh snails
1 T. salt, plus 1 t.
1 clove garlic
juice of one lemon
½ c. olive oil

Rinse the snails well and boil for 20 minutes. Remove from the flame; discard water. Add fresh hot water and a tablespoon of salt and boil for 15 more minutes.

While the snails are boiling, prepare the sauce. Mash the garlic and remaining salt together. Add the lemon juice and oil, and mix well. Remove the snails from their shells and dip in sauce.

6 SERVINGS

NOTE This is a great appetizer. Dormant snails can be bought. Soak them in cold water until they become active.

Herring Hors d'Oeuvres

Sanamura

1-2 smoked herring
2 cloves garlic
¼ c. olive oil
½ c. parsley, finely chopped
½ c. lemon juice

Debone and cut the herring into small pieces. Cut the garlic in small pieces. Mix the herring, garlic, and remaining ingredients.

4-6 SERVINGS

NOTE Serve with Arabic Bread (see page 12).

GRILLED FISH
Samak Mishwi

2 lbs. perch, ling cod, or king fish
salt
olive oil

1 Tahini Sauce recipe (see page 187)

Wash the fish; salt, and let stand for an hour. Thoroughly rub the fish with olive oil.
Grill on a charcoal grill, 15 minutes per side, and serve with tahini sauce.

6 SERVINGS

57

Fish with Pine Nut Sauce
Samak Ma(at-Taratur

3-5 lbs. perch, halibut, or cod
olive oil
salt

SAUCE
1½ c. pine nuts
2-3 large cloves garlic
salt to taste
1-1½ c. lemon juice
3 stems parsley

Rub the fish with olive oil. Wrap in heavy parchment paper that has been oiled. Bake for 30 minutes at 425° or until the fish flakes easily with a fork.

Meanwhile prepare the sauce. In a food processor, grind together the pine nuts, garlic, and salt until the nuts are of a doughlike consistency. Gradually add the lemon juice, mixing constantly until it is the consistency of yogurt.

Remove the paper from the baked fish and place the fish on a serving platter. Pour the sauce over the fish. Garnish with parsley around the edge of the fish.

6-8 SERVINGS

FISH WITH RICE
Sayyadiyyi

3-lb. whole ling cod, king fish, or perch
salt
1 c. olive oil
2 c. water
2 large onions, coarsely chopped
2 c. uncooked rice, long grain
1 T. cumin
salt and pepper to taste
2 lemons, cut into wedges

Wash the fish; salt inside and out. Let stand for 1 hour. Fry the fish in the olive oil for 3-4 minutes per side. Set on a platter. Remove the head from the fried fish and boil it in the water on a medium flame for about 30 minutes. Strain the liquid.

Brown the onions until golden brown in the fish residue, adding more olive oil if needed. Add the rice, cumin, and salt and pepper. Sauté the rice with the onions for a few minutes. Add the strained liquid plus water to measure 4 cups. Cover and cook over medium heat for 20 minutes, then simmer 10 additional minutes or until the rice is done.

Place the rice on a platter. Debone the fish and spread over the rice. Add salt and pepper to taste. Garnish with lemon wedges.

6-8 SERVINGS

MARINATED FISH FILLETS
Filetto as-Samak

2 lbs. sliced white fish fillets
1 c. olive oil
⅔ c. vinegar
1 T. butter
salt and pepper to taste
1 t. sage
1 egg
1 T. finely chopped parsley
1 c. bread crumbs
1 tomato, sliced, optional
1 lemon, cut into wedges, optional

Cover the fillets with the olive oil and vinegar (the fish should be completely covered so adjust the amount of oil and vinegar as needed). Marinate for 2 hours. Drain and place in a well-buttered baking pan. Sprinkle salt, pepper, and sage over the fish. Beat the egg well, add the parsley and pour the mixture over the top of the fish. Sprinkle bread crumbs over the entire surface. Bake at 450° for 10-15 minutes or until the fish flakes easily with a fork. Serve with tomato slices or sliced lemons.

4-6 SERVINGS

BAKED FISH SUPREME
Tajin

1 large fish (3-4 lbs.)
salt
oil

SAUCE
3 large onions, julienned
1½ c. olive oil
1 t. salt
2 t. pepper
2 c. tahini
½ c. water
1½ c. lemon juice

Clean and scale the fish (or buy cleaned and scaled). Salt inside and out. Let it stand for one hour. Grease the baking dish and the fish with oil (not necessarily olive oil). Bake the fish at 400° for 25-30 minutes or until done—when the fish will easily flake with a fork.

While the fish is baking, prepare the sauce. Sauté the onions in olive oil until golden brown. Add the salt and pepper. Mix the tahini and water thoroughly, until they thicken slightly. Gradually add the lemon juice, mixing until it becomes fluffy and thick like gravy. Add the tahini to the onions and cook over medium flame, bringing to a boil. Boil for about 10 minutes. Pour the sauce over the whole fish and bake 10 minutes more at 350°. Serve hot.

6-8 SERVINGS

NOTE This is best served with rice.

BAKED FISH
WITH TAHINI SAUCE
Samak bit-Taratur

1 large fish (3-5 lbs.)
salt
oil

SAUCE
1 clove garlic
salt to taste
1 c. *tahini*
¼ c. water
⅔ c. lemon juice
¼ c. parsley, finely chopped, plus 1 stem

Wash the fish; salt inside and out. Let it stand for one hour. Grease a baking dish and the fish with oil. Bake at 400° for 25-30 minutes or until done—when the fish flakes easily with a fork.

Prepare the sauce while the fish is baking. Mash the garlic and salt together. Add the *tahini* and mix well with a fork. Add the water and mix well. Add the lemon juice, continue mixing until it becomes thick like gravy. More water may be added if needed. Add the chopped parsley.

Remove the fish from the oven and place on a platter. Cool. Pour the sauce over the fish and garnish with parsley leaves.

6-8 SERVINGS

NOTE If the sauce is placed over hot fish, the oil in the *tahini* will separate. The fish may be deboned and served separately on a platter. The sauce is then served in a bowl with the chopped parsley on top.

SAVORY SALMON WITH SPINACH
Samak bis-Sbanikh

2-3 lbs. whole salmon
sage, fresh or dried
6 stalks of celery
2 bunches of fresh spinach
1 bunch of green onions
1 bunch of parsley
salt and pepper to taste
$\frac{1}{2}$ c. olive oil
$\frac{3}{4}$ c. water
$\frac{2}{3}$ c. fresh lemon juice

Clean the fish and rub a little sage inside the cavity. Place the fish in a roasting pan. Clean all the vegetables. Cut the celery in half lengthwise and then in $\frac{1}{2}$-inch pieces. Cover the fish with the celery. Cut the spinach in 2-inch lengths and place it on top of the celery. Dice the onions and coarsely chop the parsley. Place in that order on top of the celery. Season to taste. Pour the olive oil and water over the fish. Bake at 425° for 30 minutes. Remove the pan from the oven, stir the vegetables gently, add the lemon juice and bake for an additional 10 minutes. Serve the fish on a platter surrounded by the vegetables. The broth may be served separately.

4-6 SERVINGS

63

ENTREES
الاطباق الرئيسية

ELEGANT EGG-STUFFED MEATLOAF
Kafta Mihshi bil-Bayd

GRILLED MEAT KABOBS
Lahm Mishwi (Kabob)

GRILLED LAMB SUPREME
Shawirma

BASIC HAMBURGER A LA THE MIDDLE EAST
Kafta

GRILLED KAFTA
Kafta Mishwiyyi

KAFTA WITH PEAS
Kafta Maʿ Bazilla

BAKED KAFTA
Kafta bis-Sayniyyi

MEAT ROLLS SUPREME
Sambusik bil-Lahm

BRAIN OMELET
Ijjit an-Nkhaʿat

LEMONED LAMB LIVER
Mhamsa

GRILLED LAMB LIVER
Qasbi Mishwiyyi

RAW LIVER
Qasbi Nayyi

ARABIC SAUSAGE
Mqaniq

LAMB-VEGETABLE
CASSEROLE
Masbat ad-Darwish

OKRA WITH MEAT
Bamyi bil-Lahm

PEAS WITH LAMB
Bazilla bil-Lahm

GREEN BEANS WITH MEAT
Lubyi bil-Lahm

LAMB-ASPARAGUS
CASSEROLE
Halyun biI-Lahm

LAMB-VEGETABLE STEW
Yakhnit al Khudar bil-Lahm

POTATO STEW
Yakhnit al-batata

CRUSHED WHEAT
WITH MEAT
Burghul bid-Dfin

BAKED CHICKEN
Djaj Mhammar

EGGS FRIED WITH
CHICKEN GIBLETS
Bayd Ma' Hwahis ad-Djaj

CHICKEN WITH
VEGETABLES PAR
EXCELLENCE
Mlukhiyyi

RABBIT WITH WINE
'Arnab

SEASONED MEAT
WITH VINAIGRETTE
SAUCE
Lahm Mukhallal

MEAT WITH WHOLE
WHEAT
Harise

ROAST LEG OF LAMB
*Fakhdh aI-Ghanam
Mhammar*

PRESERVED LAMB
Qawrama

MACARONI MOLD
Qalib Ma'karuni

SPAGHETTI WITH
CUSTARD SAUCE
Ma'karuni bil-Lahm

A COUNTRY'S DIET GENERALLY CONSISTS of what is raised and grown on its terrain and that which is found in its waters. Hence the diet of the Middle East—with the Mediterranean, its rivers, and its temperate climate—consists primarily of lamb or mutton, seafood, grains, fresh vegetables, and a variety of fruits. Goat and beef products are also plentiful.

The entrees in this section are not the only entrees in this book. There are many more to try in the chapters on *Mihshi*, *Kibbi*, *Fish*, Yogurt, and Lenten dishes.

Elegant
Egg-Stuffed Meatloaf
Kafta Mihshi bil-Bayd

2 lbs. ground lamb or beef
1 large onion, grated
¼ t. cinnamon
¼ t. allspice
salt and pepper to taste
½ c. soda crackers, finely ground, or breadcrumbs
1 egg, lightly beaten
1 c. parsley, finely chopped
6 hard boiled eggs, peeled
1 T. butter

With your fingers work the onions and seasonings into the meat. Add the crackers and egg; mix thoroughly. Form the meat mixture into three loaves. Flatten the loaves until they're ½- to 1-inch thick. Sprinkle the tops of the loaves generously with parsley. Place 2 hard boiled eggs on top of the parsley. Roll as in a jelly roll, smoothing all sides. Place the loaves in a buttered baking pan and bake at 375° for 30 minutes or until brown.

67

6 SERVINGS

NOTE This is excellent for buffet dinners or as an hors d'oeuvres.

GRILLED MEAT KABOBS
Lahm Mishwi (Kabob)

2 lbs. lean lamb or beef, cut in 2-inch cubes
⅛ t. cinnamon
salt and pepper to taste
1 large onion, cut in 2-inch chunks
fresh mint

Sprinkle the meat with the seasonings. Skewer the meat and onions, alternating (3 to 1, or as desired) meat with onions. Grill over charcoal until desired tenderness. When serving, garnish with fresh mint.

6-8 SERVINGS

NOTE Meat can be marinated in ⅓ cup olive oil for an hour before grilling. Kabobs are usually eaten medium rare.

GRILLED LAMB SUPREME
Shawirma

1 lb. lamb shoulder
1 lb. leg of lamb
salt and pepper to taste

Slice the meat into 4-6-inch squares that are 1-inch thick. Alternate lean and fat pieces on the skewer of a rotisserie. As soon as the outside is cooked (to the individual's taste), slice the meat very thinly. Sprinkle with seasonings. Continue grilling and slicing as needed.

4-6 SERVINGS

NOTE This Grilled Lamb Supreme is delicious when sliced into a half loaf of Arabic Bread (see page 12). Add chopped lettuce, tomatoes, and onions. Top with Tahini Sauce (see page 187).

69

BASIC HAMBURGER A LA THE MIDDLE EAST

Kafta

1 lb. finely ground lean lamb
1 small onion, minced
½ c. finely chopped parsley
1 t. salt
¼ t. pepper
¼ t. cinnamon
⅛ t. allspice

Mix above ingredients well. Shape into hamburger-size balls. Broil or grill.

4 SERVINGS

NOTE This is a basic recipe to be used in a number of the recipes that follow.

70

GRILLED KAFTA

Kafta Mishwiyyi

1 lb. finely ground lean lamb
1 small onion, minced
½ c. finely chopped parsley
1 t. salt
¼ t. pepper
¼ t. cinnamon

Mix all of the ingredients well. Form the meat into individual long, cylinder shapes around a skewer. Broil in the oven or grill over charcoal.

4 SERVINGS

NOTE Serve with Arabic Bread (see page 12) and Yogurt (see page 173).

71

KAFTA WITH PEAS
Kafta Ma⁽ Bazilla

1 lb. finely ground lean lamb
1 small onion, minced
1 t. salt
¼ t. pepper
¼ t. cinnamon
⅛ t. allspice
1 T. butter
2 8-oz. packages of frozen peas
1 8-oz. can of tomato sauce
1 c. water
1 c. rice, cooked

Mix the lamb, onion, salt, pepper, cinnamon, and allspice well. Form the mixture into 1-inch balls. Sauté in butter. Add the frozen peas, tomato sauce, and water. Bring to boil, lower the heat and continue cooking until the peas are tender. Serve over rice.

4 SERVINGS

BAKED KAFTA
Kafta bis-Sayniyyi

1 lb. finely ground lamb or beef
1 small onion, chopped
1 egg
½ c. cracker crumbs
1½ t. salt
¼ t. pepper
¼ t. cinnamon
¼ t. allspice
4 medium potatoes
1 8-oz. can of tomato sauce
3 c. water, approximately

Thoroughly mix all of the ingredients except the potatoes, tomato sauce, and water. Form the mixture into hamburger patties about 1-inch thick. Place them next to each other in the bottom of a 9 x 12-inch pan. Peel and slice the potatoes to a thickness of ½ inch and place them over the meat. Mix the tomato sauce in about 3 cups of water and pour over the potatoes (potatoes are barely covered). Bake at 400° for 35-40 minutes.

6-8 SERVINGS

MEAT ROLLS SUPREME
Sambusik bil-Lahm

FILLING
½ c. pine nuts
2 T. butter
2 lbs. leg of lamb, finely ground
2 medium onions, finely chopped
⅛ t. cinnamon
salt and pepper to taste
½ c. lemon juice, optional

FILO
1 lb. filo dough
1 c. butter, melted

Sauté the pine nuts in 2 tablespoons of butter until golden brown. Remove the pine nuts from the butter and set aside. Sauté the meat and onions in the remainder of the butter until lightly browned. Stir in the seasonings and pine nuts. Cool. (If a tart flavor is desired, add lemon juice and mix ingredients well.) Take 2 sheets of filo dough and brush the tops with the melted butter. Place the filling (in the thickness of a cigar) on the buttered side along the long edge to within 1-inch of both ends. Roll the dough one turn over the filling. Turn the 2 short ends of the dough toward center to secure the meat in the roll and continue rolling as for a jelly roll. Repeat for the second sheet of filo.

Arrange the rolls on buttered baking pan, brush the tops lightly with butter and bake in a preheated oven at 400° or until the dough is lightly browned. Slice the rolls into the desired length before serving.

6-8 SERVINGS

NOTE Excellent for hors d'oeuvres.

BRAIN OMELET
Ijjit an-Nkha'at

1 lb. lamb or beef brains
2 t. salt, plus salt and pepper to taste
1 T. lemon juice
4 eggs
½ c. parsley, finely chopped
1 small onion, finely chopped

Rinse the brains thoroughly. Place the brains, salt, lemon juice, and enough water to cover in a pan. Bring to a boil and cook until a fork pierces the meat easily. Drain and devein the brains and chop.

Beat the eggs and add the parsley. Add the onions after sprinkling them with the salt and pepper. Add the chopped brain and carefully mix. Place in a greased 7-inch pan that has been heated. Bake at 375° for 15-20 minutes or until done, when the brains are firm to the touch.

4 SERVINGS

75

LEMONED LAMB LIVER
Mhamsa

1 lb. lamb liver
2 medium onions, chopped
2 T. olive oil
salt and pepper to taste
¼ c. lemon juice

Cut the liver into 1-inch pieces. Sauté the onions in the oil until limp. Add the liver and seasonings and continue sautéing for a few minutes. Add the lemon juice and water to barely cover. Bring to a quick boil. Lower the heat and simmer for about 5 minutes. This must be cooked rapidly—10 minutes maximum cooking time.

4 SERVINGS

76

GRILLED LAMB LIVER
Qasbi Mishwiyyi

1 lb. lamb liver
2 onions
salt and pepper to taste
cherry tomatoes, optional

Cut the liver and onions into 2-inch chunks. Sprinkle with salt and pepper. Alternate liver, onions, and tomatoes on skewers. Grill on charcoal for 5-7 minutes, or until done, turning constantly.

4 SERVINGS

77

RAW LIVER
Qasbi Nayyi

1 lb. lamb liver
salt and pepper to taste
1 bunch of green onions, sliced

Cut the liver into 1-inch cubes. Place on a platter and sprinkle with salt and pepper
(cayenne pepper may be substituted). Serve with the green onion.

4 SERVINGS

NOTE Raw liver is eaten from a freshly butchered sheep only. This is excellent as
an appetizer.

78

ARABIC SAUSAGE
Mqaniq

STUFFING

2 lbs. lean lamb, coarsely ground

2 lbs. pork, coarsely ground

2 c. sweet red wine

½ c. coriander seed

2 T. allspice

1 T. cinnamon

salt and pepper to taste

lamb or pork casing

Mix all of the stuffing ingredients thoroughly. Refrigerate for 3-4 hours, stirring occasionally. Stuff the filling into the casing, using a 1-inch funnel slipped into the casing as a guide to insert the sausage mixture. With thread, tie off the sausages at the desired length. Age by hanging in a cold place or refrigerate for two days before freezing. To serve, cut into links and fry or grill.

8 SERVINGS

NOTE If casing is unavailable, refrigerate for 24 hours, then make into patties or rolls and freeze.

LAMB-VEGETABLE CASSEROLE
Masbat ad-Darwish

1 lb. lamb shoulder, cut into 1-inch chunks
2 large potatoes
2 small eggplants, or 1 large
3 tomatoes
2 zucchini
2 medium onions
¼ t. cinnamon
salt and pepper to taste

Sauté the lamb until lightly browned. Peel the potatoes and eggplants. Rinse. Cut all of the vegetables in ½-inch slices lengthwise then cut them into ½-inch pieces. Arrange all the ingredients in alternating layers in a 9 x 12-inch pan. Begin with the potatoes, then zucchini, meat, eggplant, tomatoes, and onions last. Sprinkle the seasonings on top. Barely cover with water. Cover and bake at 375° for 35-40 minutes. Uncover for the last 10 minutes for browning.

6 SERVINGS

NOTE This is usually served with rice.

OKRA WITH MEAT
Bamyi bil-Lahm

1 lb. fresh tender okra
1 T. olive oil
¾ lb. lamb shoulder, coarsely ground
1 medium onion, chopped
2 cloves garlic, chopped
1 t. ground coriander or 2 t. coriander seed
salt and pepper to taste
1 c. water
1 8-oz. can tomato sauce
½-¾ c. lemon juice

Rinse the okra and cut off the stems. Dry. Sauté the okra in olive oil until lightly brown. (The okra may be brushed with butter or margarine and placed under the broiler to brown.) Set aside.

Sauté the meat in the leftover oil for about 5 minutes, stirring constantly. Add the onions, garlic, and seasonings and continue sautéing until the onions are limp. Add the water and simmer for 15 minutes. Then add the tomato sauce and lemon juice (add more lemon juice if you prefer a tart taste). Add the okra and gently stir the mixture once. (Do not stir it again.) Cook for 10-15 minutes or until the okra is tender.

4 SERVINGS

NOTE Frozen okra may be substituted. Omit the sautéing.

Peas with Lamb
Bazilla bil-Lahm

1 lb. tender young peas and pods
1 lb. lamb shoulder, coarsely ground
⅛ t. cinnamon
salt and pepper to taste
1 large onion, chopped
2 c. water
2 tomatoes or 1 8-oz. can tomato sauce

Shell the peas and save the soft outside portion of the pea pod. (This is done by bending the pod in half lengthwise, which will split the pod in half. From the split, peel off the soft portions.)

Brown the meat with the seasonings. Add the onions and sauté until golden. Add the water and simmer for 15 minutes. Add the tomatoes or tomato sauce and cook for 10 minutes more. Add the peas and pods and let simmer for 15 minutes.

4 SERVINGS

NOTE Canned or frozen peas may be substituted. Pods will be omitted. Adjust the cooking time per the package instructions.

GREEN BEANS WITH MEAT
Lubyi bil-Lahm

2 lbs. fresh green beans
1 lb. lamb shoulder
2 medium onions, chopped
2 cloves garlic, chopped
$\frac{1}{8}$ t. cinnamon
salt and pepper to taste
$\frac{1}{4}$ c. water
1 8-oz. can tomato sauce, or 3 medium-sized fresh tomatoes, finely chopped

Clean, stem, and cut the beans in about 2-inch lengths and set aside.

Cut the meat into 1-inch cubes and sauté for 10 minutes. Add the onions, garlic, and seasonings; sauté for 5 minutes more. Add the water and simmer for 10 minutes. Add the beans and tomatoes; toss. Add water to half the depth of the meat and bean mixture. Cover and cook for 20-25 minutes on a medium flame or until the beans and meat are tender. Stir occasionally.

4 SERVINGS

NOTE Canned or frozen beans may be substituted.

83

Lamb-Asparagus Casserole
Halyun bil-Lahm

1 lb. fresh asparagus
½ lb. lamb shoulder, coarsely chopped
1 clove garlic, chopped, optional
1 medium onion, chopped
⅛ t. cinnamon
⅛ t. allspice
salt and pepper to taste
2 T. butter
1 c. water

Cut tender asparagus into 2-inch lengths. Rinse, drain, and set aside. Sauté the meat, garlic, onions, and seasonings in butter. Add the asparagus and simmer for 5 minutes. Add the water and cook for about 20-25 minutes or until tender.

4 SERVINGS

NOTE This can also be cooked in a covered casserole and baked for 15-20 minutes at 400°. Serve with rice.

84

LAMB-VEGETABLE STEW
Yakhnit al Khudar bil-Lahm

2 stalks of celery
3 carrots
2 potatoes
2 turnips
1 parsnip
1 large onion
1 lb. lamb, cut into $1\frac{1}{2}$-inch cubes
2 cloves garlic, minced
$\frac{1}{8}$ t. allspice
salt and pepper to taste

Cut all of the vegetables into 2-inch lengths. Place all of the ingredients in a pot and cover with water to 2 inches above the ingredients. Cover and cook on a medium flame for 45-50 minutes, until the meat is tender, stirring occasionally. Add additional water if needed.

4 SERVINGS

POTATO STEW
Yakhnit al-batata

1 lb. lamb shoulder, cubed
⅛ t. cinnamon
salt and pepper to taste
1 large onion, chopped
4 large potatoes, peeled and cut into small chunks
1 8-oz. can of tomato sauce

Sauté the meat and seasonings slowly for a few minutes in a saucepan. Add the onions and potatoes. Toss with a closed lid. Slowly cook covered for 10 minutes on a low flame. Add the tomato sauce and water to half the depth of the ingredients. Simmer until done, 20-30 minutes.

4 SERVINGS

CRUSHED WHEAT WITH MEAT
Burghul bi∂-Dfin

1½ lbs. shank or 1 lb. stew meat, cut in chunks
1 large onion, cut in chunks
1 T. olive oil
2½ c. water
1 c. *burghul*, #3
1 15-oz. can garbanzo beans, drained
½ t. cinnamon
1½ t. salt

Brown the meat and onions in the oil, then transfer to a pot with water to cover the meat and cook until the meat is almost tender, 30-40 minutes. Remove the *zafra* (fat curds) as it forms. Remove the meat from the broth and debone. Return the meat to the measured water and add the *burghul*, garbanzos, and seasonings. Cook until the *burghul* is done and is the consistency of cooked rice, about 20 minutes. (Add additional water if needed.)

87

4 SERVINGS

NOTE If stew meat is used, brown the meat and onions in a small amount of oil and continue cooking until almost tender. Proceed as above.

BAKED CHICKEN
Djaj Mhammar

¼ c. olive oil
¼ c. lemon juice
1 t. salt
1 t. oregano
½ t. pepper
¼ t. cinnamon, plus cinnamon to taste
1 chicken, fryer, cut into serving-sized pieces
1 c. uncooked rice

Combine the olive oil, lemon juice, and spices in a shallow baking pan. Roll the cut-up chicken in the marinade. Bake at 425°, basting occasionally, until tender when pierced with a fork (approximately 30 minutes). Meanwhile prepare the rice per the package instructions.

Remove the chicken from the oven and baste again. Sprinkle the rice with cinnamon. Serve the chicken around a bed of rice. The chicken juices may be served in separate bowl to pour over the rice.

4 SERVINGS

VARIATION

To make *Djaj Mishwi* (Grilled Chicken), prepare the chicken as above without the seasonings. Grill the chicken over charcoal and serve with *Tum biz-Zayt* (Garlic Sauce)—see page 189. Dip the chicken pieces in the sauce.

Eggs Fried with Chicken Giblets

Bayd Ma'Hwahis ad-Djaj

¼ lb. giblets (or giblets of one chicken)
oil or butter
3 eggs
salt and pepper to taste

Cut the gizzards and heart into small chunks. Sauté in the oil or butter, then add the liver; sauté until tender. Add the eggs and seasonings to the giblets and cook like an omelet; or the eggs may be left whole on top of the giblets.

3 SERVINGS

NOTE In the Middle East, this is usually served for breakfast but is excellent for lunch or any other time.

89

Chicken with Vegetables Par Excellence
Mlukhiyyi

1 chicken, fryer, or 4 lamb shanks
⅛ t. cinnamon
salt and pepper to taste
2 large onions, finely chopped
1 c. vinegar with ¼ c. water
2 lbs. *mlukhiyyi*, fresh or 1 lb. dry
2 loaves Arabic Bread (see page 12), toasted until golden brown
2 c. rice, cooked

Place the chicken and seasonings in a pot and cover with water. Cook until the chicken is tender, about 45 minutes. Remove the chicken and debone. Place in a serving dish and keep warm. Set the broth aside.

Meanwhile, cover the onions with the vinegar and water. Add a dash of salt and pepper. Soak for 45 minutes. If fresh *mlukhiyyi* is used, chop the leaves razor-thin. Add *mlukhiyyi* in the chicken broth and cook for 15 minutes. Place in a soup tureen.

Break the toasted bread into 1-inch pieces. To serve, place a handful of bread in the bottom of each individual soup bowl or plate. Place a scoop of onions with a little juice over the bread; add the desired amount of rice and top with a scoop of the *mlukhiyyi* and chicken.

4-6 SERVINGS

NOTE Check your local market for this green leafy vegetable, *mlukhiyyi*. In the Middle East, it is available in the winter and early spring.

RABBIT WITH WINE
’Arnab

1 rabbit, cut into pieces
1 c. oil
4-6 small whole onions, peeled
¾ c. red wine
¼ c. vinegar
¾ c. water
salt and pepper to taste
cinnamon to taste

Fry the individual pieces of rabbit in hot oil until golden brown. Place in a covered baking dish. Place the onions on top of the rabbit. Pour the wine, vinegar, water, and seasonings over the rabbit and onions. Simmer on a low flame or in the oven for 1 hour.

4-6 SERVINGS

NOTE Serve with plain rice.

91

SEASONED MEAT WITH VINAIGRETTE SAUCE

Lahm Mukhallal

1 chicken or rabbit
4 T. olive oil
2 large onions, julienned
1 T. flour
⅓-½ c. white vinegar
2 c. tomato sauce
1 c. water
2 t. pickling spice
2 t. salt
⅛ t. pepper
⅛ t. allspice

Cut the chicken or rabbit into serving-size pieces. Fry the meat in olive oil until golden brown and place in a 6 quart pan so the meat is no more than 2 layers deep.

Sauté the onions until limp, and place them on top of the meat. Sprinkle the flour over the residue in the bottom of the pan and blend. Add the vinegar (quantity dependent on tartness desired), tomato sauce, and water; pour the mixture over the meat to barely cover. Tie the pickling spice in a cheese cloth and add this with the remaining spices to the liquid. If cheese cloth is unavailable, then add the pickling spice directly and remove when done. Simmer about an hour or until tender.

SERVES 4

NOTE Beef or lamb may be substituted; use red wine vinegar instead of white. The meat should be almost done before placing the onions on top. The liquid may be reduced.

MEAT WITH WHOLE WHEAT

Harise

2 lbs. lamb shanks
1 stick cinnamon
salt and pepper to taste
2 c. whole wheat kernels
2 c. plain yogurt

In a deep pan, completely cover the meat with cold water, add seasonings, bring to boil and remove the *zafra* (fat curd). Continue simmering until the meat is just tender. Rinse the whole wheat kernels, then add to the meat. Bring to a boil, reduce the heat to medium and stir constantly until it has the consistency of gravy. Remove from the heat, debone the meat, and return it to the wheat mixture. Mix and serve with plain yogurt.

SERVES 6

93

ROAST LEG OF LAMB
Fakhdh al-Ghanam Mhammar

5-6 lbs. leg of lamb
⅛ t. cinnamon
⅛ t. allspice
salt and freshly ground pepper to taste
4-5 cloves garlic, peeled

Rub the seasonings over the meat. Make pockets in the meat by piercing it with a knife. Insert the garlic cloves into the pockets. Place the leg of lamb on a rack in shallow roasting pan. For a medium roast, bake at 300° for 30 minutes per pound or until the meat thermometer registers 160°.

10 SERVINGS

NOTE The garlic may be reduced according to individual taste. Gravy can be made from the drippings and served over rice.

PRESERVED LAMB
Qawrama

1 lb. lamb shoulder, finely ground
salt and pepper to taste

Place the meat in a pot. Add salt (should be on the salty side) and pepper to taste. Cook on high heat for a few minutes. Lower the heat to medium and continue cooking, stirring occasionally. When the fat is completely rendered, about 30-45 minutes, and the meat is light brown, *qawrama* is ready. Pour the meat in a wide-mouth glass or earthenware jar. Cover and refrigerate. A fat layer will form on top.

6 SERVINGS

NOTE Use this in preparation for various other dishes. Scoop both the fat and the meat from the container and serve with fried eggs or *kishk*. It's also good when cooked with vegetables.

95

MACARONI MOLD
Qalib Ma'karuni

¾ lb. spaghetti
1 T. butter, plus 2 T.
¼ c. bread crumbs
⅓ c. pine nuts
1 lb. ground beef or lamb
1 large onion, finely chopped
2 large cloves garlic, finely chopped
salt and pepper to taste
2 8-oz. cans tomato sauce

Cook the spaghetti in boiling salted water until tender. Thoroughly drain. Generously butter an angel food or a bundt pan and dust with fine bread crumbs.

Sauté the pine nuts in butter until golden brown. Add the meat, onions, and garlic and continue sautéing until the meat is lightly browned. Add seasonings and tomato sauce. Simmer for 10 minutes.

Place half of the spaghetti in the prepared pan. Layer one half of the meat mixture on top of spaghetti. Add the remaining spaghetti and top with the meat mixture. Sprinkle with additional bread crumbs.

Bake at 350° for 30 minutes. Remove from the oven and let stand in the pan for 5 minutes. Turn onto a platter and leave the mold on for an additional 5 minutes. Remove the mold and serve.

6-8 SERVINGS

Spaghetti with Custard Sauce

Ma'karuni bil-Lahm

1 lb. spaghetti
1/3 c. pine nuts
1 T. butter, plus additional for pan
1 lb. ground beef or lamb
1/8 t. cinnamon
1/8 t. allspice
salt and pepper to taste

SAUCE

2 eggs, well beaten
4 c. milk
1 T. corn starch

Cook the spaghetti in salted boiling water, drain, and set aside. Brown the pine nuts in the butter. Add the meat and seasonings and continue sautéing until brown. Butter a 9 x 13-inch pan. Place 1 layer of spaghetti on the bottom. Spread the meat on top and place the remaining spaghetti on top of the meat mixture.

Thoroughly mix all of the sauce ingredients with a fork. Pour over the spaghetti and bake at 350° for 30-35 minutes, until the mixture sets.

6-8 SERVINGS

KIBBI
الكبة

POTATO-WALNUT SUPREME
Kibbit Batata bij-Jawz

MONK'S KIBBI
Kibbit ar-Rahib

PUMPKIN KIBBI
Kibbit Laqtin

KIBBI IN YOGURT SAUCE
Kibbi bil-Laban

GRILLED OR BARBECUED
KIBBI
Kibbi Mishwiyyi

RAW KIBBI
Kibbi Nayyi

KIBBI IS ONE OF THE PRIZES of Lebanese cuisine and is served largely on special occasions. *Kibbi*, colloquial for *kubaybah*, is in fact renowned among all Middle Eastern dishes. The word comes from the verb that means to form into a ball. With the exception of *Kibbi bis-Sayniyyi* (Baked Kibbi), a ball of the mixture is used in shaping the desired forms; that is, spheres, patties, domes, etc. The basic ingredients for *kibbi* are *burghul*, or crushed wheat, and meat. Before the days of meat grinders and now food processors, the meat was pounded by hand—a process requiring much time and effort. From these two simple ingredients, a variety of gourmet dishes are made. *Kibbi* can be served raw, but is most often cooked. If you're preparing a recipe to be served raw, be sure to buy the finest quality meat. *Kibbi* can be served as an entree, an hors d'oeuvre, or as a Lenten or vegetarian dish.

This chapter begins with two basic recipes, one for *Kibbi* and one for Basic *Kibbi* Stuffing. Neither includes serving information because these two recipes will serve as a base for most of the *kibbi* recipes in this chapter.

HINTS

~ Leg of lamb is the preferred meat in *kibbi*, but lean beef (such as ground round) may be substituted.

~ *Kibbi* should have enough salt when cooked, fried, or baked to prevent it from falling apart in the cooking process.

~ For the best results, the ratio of meat to *burghul* is $1\frac{1}{2}$ to 1.

~ When making *Kibbi bis-Sayniyyi*, if there is excessive shrinking from the sides of the pan ($\frac{1}{2}$ inch or more), not enough *burghul* was used. If need be, adjust the amount of *burghul*.

~ When using rinsed *burghul* that is to be set aside 10-15 minutes, be sure to sprinkle it with salt to prevent it from getting mushy.

~ When using *kibbi*, unstuffed, it is best to leave a pocket in the center of the *kibbi* ball so that it will cook through.

~ If there is excess *kibbi* or stuffing, *kibbi* may be fried into patties and the stuffing may be scrambled with eggs.

~ *Burghul* #2 is generally used in most *kibbi* recipes. A personal preference of #1, which is finer, or #3, which is coarser, is left to the cook.

~ *Burghul* #3 is usually preferred for all other dishes.

~ When heating frozen *kibbi*, brush or dot the top of the *kibbi* with additional butter for a fresh taste and texture.

~ If preparing a recipe that calls for serving the meat raw, it's best to work with a good butcher to assure you get the finest quality meat.

BASIC KIBBI
Kibbi

2⅔ c. *burghul*, plus ½ c. when using lamb
1 large onion, grated
2 T. salt
¼ t. pepper
⅛ t. cinnamon
⅛ t. allspice
2 lbs. ground lean lamb or beef

Cover the *burghul* with cold water. Soak for 10 minutes. Drain and press the *burghul* between the palms of your hands to remove any excess water. Work the onions and spices together with your fingers. Knead the meat and spices thoroughly; add the crushed wheat and continue kneading. Dip your hands in ice water while kneading in order to soften the *kibbi*. (The ingredients must be kept cold.) Run the kneaded mixture through a food processor one to three times for a finer consistency.

8 SERVINGS

NOTE This Basic *Kibbi* recipe along with the Basic *Kibbi* Stuffing will serve as the starter for many of the *kibbi* recipes that follow. When using beef, ¼ teaspoon of ground sweet basil may be added.

BASIC KIBBI STUFFING
Hashwit al-Kibbi

¼ c. pine nuts
2 T. butter
½ lb. ground lamb shoulder
1 medium onion, finely chopped
⅛ t. cinnamon
⅛ t. allspice
salt and pepper to taste

Brown the pine nuts in the butter until golden, then add the meat and sauté for 10-12 minutes. Add the onions and spices and cook until the onions are limp. Remove from the heat.

8 SERVINGS

NOTE This Basic *Kibbi* Stuffing recipe along with the Basic *Kibbi* recipe will serve as the starter for many of the *kibbi* recipes that follow.

FRIED KIBBI PATTIES
Kibbi Miqliyyi

½ Basic *Kibbi* recipe (see page 102)

Shape the meat mixture like hamburger patties and fry in a skillet. Or place the patties in a buttered or oiled pan and baked at 400° for 20 minutes or until well browned. Turn the patties once during baking.

4 SERVINGS

STUFFED KIBBI SPHERES
Kibbi Mihshiyyi

½ Basic *Kibbi* recipe (see page 102)
1 Basic *Kibbi* Stuffing recipe (see page 103)

Place a walnut-sized chunk of *kibbi* in the palm of your hand. Using your forefinger, press a hole in the *kibbi* and begin expanding the hole by rotating your finger and pressing the *kibbi* against the palm of your hand until the shell is ¼-inch thick. Place a teaspoonful of stuffing into the hole. Carefully close the hole, forming a football-shaped sphere. (Use cold water on your hands to help shape and close the balls.)

Arrange the *kibbi* spheres in a well-buttered or well-oiled pan and bake at 375° for 20-30 minutes, turning occasionally until browned.

8-10 SERVINGS, 3 DOZEN

NOTE Walnut-sized chunks make about 2-inch spheres. This is a nice size for hors d'oeuvres or for a buffet. For 3-4-inch spheres, use a heaping tablespoon. Other shapes and sizes can be made. *Kibbi* spheres may also be stuffed with a few pine nuts, sautéed pine nuts with chopped onions, lamb suet pounded with spices and onions, or made hollow without stuffing.

KIBBI IN KISHK
Kibbi bil-Kishk

½ Basic *Kibbi* recipe (see page 102)
1 Basic *Kibbi* Stuffing recipe (see page 103)

1 medium onion, chopped
2-3 cloves garlic, chopped
¼ c. butter
2 c. *kishk*
6-8 c. water
salt and pepper to taste

Form the *kibbi* into 2½-inch football-shaped spheres and stuff (see page 104). Set aside.

Sauté the onion and garlic in butter in a heavy pan. Gradually add the *kishk* and sauté in the butter mixture, stirring constantly. Slowly add the water. Bring to a boil, stirring constantly. Add salt and pepper to taste. Cover and simmer for 15 minutes. Bring to a boil and add the *kibbi* balls. Simmer for an additional 15 minutes. (When thickened, this should be the consistency of medium gravy. Add water if needed.) Serve like stew, allowing 3-4 *kibbi* balls per serving.

8-10 SERVINGS

105

NOTE *Kishk* is made from yogurt and *burghul* that has been ground, fermented, and salted. It has the texture of corn meal and can be found in Middle Eastern shops. *Kibbi* in *Kishk* can also be served over rice.

Supreme Lamb Stew with Kibbi

Kibbi Qarnabiyyi

½ Basic *Kibbi* recipe (see page 102)
1 Basic *Kibbi* Stuffing recipe (see page 103)

2 lbs. of boned lamb, shank, shoulder, or leg, cubed in 2-inch pieces
⅛ t. pepper
⅛ t. cinnamon
⅛ t. allspice
salt to taste
2 large onions, julienned
1 15-oz. can garbanzo beans, drained
1½ c. sesame seed oil (*tahini*)
¼ c. water
juice of 4 lemons (1⅓ c.)
juice of 2 large grapefruits (⅔ c.)

Form the *kibbi* into 2-3-inch spherical shapes and stuff (see page 104). Set aside.

Place the meat and seasonings in a pot. Completely cover with cold water. Cover and cook on a medium flame for about 45 minutes. Add the onions and garbanzo beans, lower to simmer and cook for 10 minutes. Remove from the flame and cool.

Thoroughly mix the sesame seed oil with the water. Add the lemon and grapefruit juice. Blend well with a mixer until it's fluffy like cream. If it's too thick, add a little more water.

Gradually add the sauce to the meat and liquid, stirring constantly. Cook on a medium flame, stirring 2 or 3 times, until it comes to a boil. Then gently add the *kibbi* spheres so as not to break them. Bring to a boil. Cook 15-20 minutes more.

10-12 SERVINGS

NOTE Serve on a bed of plain cooked rice.

FISH KIBBI
Kibbit Samak

2 c. *burghul*

1 T. salt

½ c. pine nuts

½ c. oil, plus ⅓ c., plus ½ c.

2 large onions, julienned

1 medium onion, grated

1 T. ground coriander or ½ bunch of chopped green coriander,
     or 1 T. sweet basil may be substituted

1 orange rind, grated

⅛ t. pepper

1½ lbs. boned white fish

Wash the *burghul* in cold water, squeeze, sprinkle with salt, and set aside.

Sauté the pine nuts in ½ cup of the oil until golden brown. Add the julienned onions and continue sautéing until the onions are limp. Set aside.

Thoroughly mix the grated onion with the coriander, orange rind, and pepper. Grind the raw fish in a food processor. Combine the fish with the onion and coriander mixture. Blend with your fingers. Add the *burghul* and knead until it's the consistency of dough, dipping your hands in cold water to soften the mixture.

Grease a 9-inch square pan with ⅓ cup of the oil. Spread a ½-inch layer of fish *kibbi* on the bottom of the pan. (It is easier to take a large ball, pat it flat, place it in the pan, and piece the *kibbi* where needed.) Smooth the *kibbi* out evenly with your hands. Spread the sautéed julienned onions and pine nuts evenly on top of the fish mixture. Place the rest of the *kibbi* mixture on top of the onions, spreading evenly. Score the top layer ½-inch deep in 1-inch diamond shapes.

Pour the remaining ½ cup of oil evenly over the top and bake in 400° oven for 35-45 minutes until golden brown.

4-6 SERVINGS

NOTE This is an excellent Lenten dish. This recipe can be made into patties. Fry or bake in a well-oiled pan. Omit the onion and pine nut stuffing.

BAKED KIBBI
Kibbi bis-Sayniyyi

butter
1 Basic *Kibbi* recipe (see page 102)
1 Basic *Kibbi* Stuffing recipe (see page 103)
½ c. melted butter

Generously butter a 9 x 12-inch cake pan. Spread a ½-inch layer of *kibbi* on the bottom of the pan. Leave enough of the *kibbi* so the top layer will be thicker than the bottom. (It is easier to take several large balls, pat them flat, place them in the pan, piecing the *kibbi* to form an even layer on the bottom of the pan.) Smooth the *kibbi* out evenly with your hands. Spread the stuffing evenly over the *kibbi*. Then spread the remaining *kibbi* mixture on top, using the same method as with the bottom layer. Smooth well.

Score the top layer ½-inch deep in 1-inch diamond shapes. Pour the melted butter over the top. Bake in a 400° oven for 25 minutes, lower the heat to 300°, and bake for 20-30 minutes more until golden brown. When serving, cut along the diamond-shaped wedges.

8-10 SERVINGS

POTATO KIBBI
Kibbit Batata bis-Sayniyyi

1½ c. *burghul*, #2
2 t. salt
1 T. sweet basil
⅛ t. cinnamon
⅛ t. pepper
1 small onion, grated
4 medium potatoes, cooked and mashed
2 large onions, julienned
⅔ c. oil

Rinse the *burghul* in cold water, squeeze, sprinkle with salt, and let stand for 20 minutes. Work the seasonings in with the grated onion, then add the potatoes, mixing well. Add the *burghul* and knead into a soft dough. If need be, moisten your hands in cold water while kneading to prevent sticking. (If the mixture does not stick together, add ¼ cup of flour.)

Place the julienned onions in the bottom of a 9-inch square pan. Cover with ⅓ cup of the oil. Place the potato mixture evenly on top and cut ½-inch deep diamond shapes on the surface. Pour the remaining oil on top and bake at 400° until golden brown, about 25 minutes.

6-8 SERVINGS

NOTE You can use this recipe, omitting the oil and julienned onions, to form patties. Fry the patties in ½-inch of oil or put them in a well-oiled pan and bake.

POTATO-WALNUT SUPREME
Kibbit Batata bij-Jawz

½ c. *burghul*, #1
4 medium potatoes, cooked and mashed
¾-1 c. walnuts, finely ground
1 large onion, finely grated
⅛ t. cinnamon
salt and pepper to taste
¼ c. chopped mint, parsley, or radishes

Cover and soak the *burghul* in cold water for 15-20 minutes.

Combine the potatoes, walnuts, onions, and seasonings. Drain the *burghul* by squeezing well and add it to the mixture. Thoroughly mix all the ingredients and grind in a food processor. If the mixture is too firm, add cold water. Knead by hand until the mixture resembles a soft dough.

Place on a platter and score with a fork. Garnish with mint, parsley, or radishes. This dish may be served cold or at room temperature.

2-4 SERVINGS

MONK'S KIBBI
Kibbit ar-Rahib

1 c. dried lentils
7 c. water
1 medium onion, coarsely chopped
salt and pepper to taste
3 T. olive oil

KIBBI
½ c. *burghul*, #2
2 T. flour
1 small onion, minced
1 t. sweet basil
salt and pepper to taste
1 lemon, cut into wedges

111

Rinse the lentils, add the water, onions, seasonings, and olive oil. Cover and cook for about 15 minutes.

Rinse the *burghul* in cold water. Drain by squeezing tightly. Thoroughly mix all the *kibbi* ingredients except the lemon. The mixture will be sticky but can be formed into 1-inch balls; add more flour if necessary. Drop the balls gently into the boiling lentil mixture and continue cooking for 15-20 minutes. Serve with lemon wedges.

2-4 SERVINGS

Pumpkin Kibbi
Kibbit Laqtin

2 c. *burghul*
1 t. salt
1 small onion, grated
1 T. coriander seed or ½ bunch of fresh coriander
⅛ t. pepper
3 c. mashed, cooked fresh pumpkin
⅓ c. flour
⅔ c. oil
2 large onions, julienned

Wash the *burghul* in cold water, squeeze, sprinkle with salt, and set aside.

Mix the onion with the coriander and pepper, then mix well with the cooled, cooked pumpkin. Add the *burghul* and knead well like dough, adding the flour as needed to hold the ingredients together.

Cover the bottom of a 9-inch square pan with ⅓ cup of the oil and the julienned onions. Pat the *burghul* mixture on top carefully, then cut a 1-inch diamond or square design—make the cuts ¼-inch deep—on the surface. Pour the rest of the oil on top and bake at 400° for 25-30 minutes until golden brown. To serve, cut along the lines to the size desired.

8 SERVINGS

KIBBI IN YOGURT SAUCE
Kibbi bil-Laban

½ Basic *Kibbi* recipe (see page 102), makes about 1½ dozen *kibbi* spheres
1 Basic *Kibbi* Stuffing recipe (see page 103), optional

2 eggs or 2 T. cornstarch dissolved in water
2 quarts plain yogurt
2 c. water
1 clove garlic
1 T. dry mint or 2 T. fresh mint
1½ t. salt
¼ c. butter

Place a walnut-sized chunk of *kibbi* in the palm of your hand and form it into a foot-ball-shaped sphere. If using the optional Basic *Kibbi* Stuffing, before forming it into a sphere, use your forefinger to press a hole in the *kibbi*. Expand the hole by rotating your finger and pressing the *kibbi* against the palm of your hand until the shell is ¼-inch thick. Place a teaspoon of the stuffing into the hole then carefully close it, forming a football-shaped sphere. Repeat until the *kibbi* and *kibbi* stuffing are gone.

Beat the eggs in a saucepan until foamy. Add the yogurt and stir constantly over medium heat for 8-10 minutes. Add the water and continue stirring constantly until the *laban* comes to a fast boil. Lower the heat and add the *kibbi* balls—do not stir.

Crush the garlic and mix in the mint and salt. Sauté the mixture in butter for 5-8 minutes. Add the garlic and mint mixture to the yogurt mixture, stirring once gently. Taste for flavor and correct with salt. Continue cooking on medium heat for 15-20 minutes. (The *laban* will be like thick gravy.)

8-10 SERVINGS

NOTE Serve with rice.

GRILLED OR BARBECUED KIBBI
Kibbi Mishwiyyi

1 Basic *Kibbi* recipe (see page 102)
1 Basic *Kibbi* Stuffing recipe (see page 103), optional

Form 2 hamburger-sized patties about ½-inch thick with the *kibbi*. Place a table-spoon of stuffing on the bottom patty. Cup the top patty in your hand and place it over the filling, forming a dome shape. Press the edges of the 2 patties together. Grill for 15-20 minutes or until cooked through.

6-8 SERVINGS

NOTE Other shapes can be made with or without the stuffing.

RAW KIBBI
Kibbi Nayyi

1 c. *burghul*, #1
1 T. salt
⅛ t. pepper
⅛ t. cinnamon
⅛ t. allspice
2 medium onions, grated
1 lb. lamb, very lean and freshly butchered, finely ground
olive oil
⅛ c. fresh mint or parsley

Rinse the *burghul* well and squeeze out the excess water. Sprinkle with salt, toss, cover, and refrigerate for approximately 20-25 minutes.

Work the remaining seasonings into the grated onions with your fingers, then mix the onions into the meat with your hands. Add the chilled *burghul* to the mixture, kneading well until it's a soft consistency. Dip your hands in cold water to ensure a soft consistency. Grind in a food processor 1 to 3 times for a finer consistency.

Spread on a platter. (Spreading is done by pressing and pulling with outstretched fingers to flatten the mixture against the platter. This leaves a pattern of finger imprints in the *kibbi*.) Olive oil may be poured over the top or served separately in a small container. Garnish with fresh mint or parsley.

8-10 SERVINGS

NOTE This is a favorite appetizer and is renowned throughout the Middle East. If the *kibbi* is to be eaten right away, soak the *burghul* in ice water for 15 minutes. After squeezing out the excess water, work all the seasonings into the onions. Proceed as above. Choice lean beef may be used. Add ½ teaspoon of ground sweet basil when beef is substituted.

MIHSHI
المحشي

STUFFED GRAPE LEAVES
Mihshi Waraq 'Inab

STUFFED CABBAGE LEAVES
Mihshi Malfuf

STUFFED ARTICHOKE
'Ardishawki bil-Lahm

STUFFED EGGPLANT SUPREME
Shaykh al-Mihshi

STUFFED ZUCCHINI
Kusa Mihshi

STUFFED ZUCCHINI SUPREME
'Ablama

STUFFED RIBS AND SOUP
Dil' Mihshi

STUFFED CHICKEN AND SOUP
Djaj Mihshi

STUFFED TURKEY
Habash Mihshi

STUFFED TRIPE
AND CASING SUPREME
Ghammi

STUFFED POTATOES
Mihshi Batata

MIHSHI COMES FROM THE ARABIC verb that means to stuff, denoting a preparation of food that is stuffed. This section of recipes is dedicated to this category of dish, which is made of meats and vegetables with a simple filling that consists basically of ground meat, rice, and spices.

The vegetables typically used in *mihshi* are grape, cabbage, and Swiss chard leaves. Also included are potatoes, eggplants, green peppers, zucchini, and artichokes. The favorite meats used in *mihshi* are chicken and lamb or beef ribs. *Mihshi* is a particularly succulent dish with a variety of seasonings that enhance each vegetable or meat used.

HINTS

~ In *mihshi* dishes, long grain white rice is preferable.

~ Although finely chopped meat is preferred, ground meat may be substituted.

~ Shoulder lamb is most commonly used for *mihshi* dishes, but ground chuck may be substituted.

~ Of interest: cinnamon is used with all fowl and meats to mask the *zankhit al-lahm* or the particular meaty flavor.

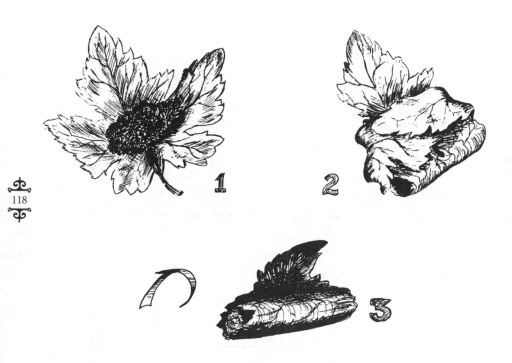

VARIATIONS

Use 2 large eggplants, cut in $\frac{1}{2}$-inch rounds. Lightly grease the pan with olive oil. Layer the bottom of the pan with raw eggplant. Put 1-2 tablespoons of filling on each round. If additional filling and eggplant remains, continue layering. Then proceed with the tomato sauce, water, and salt and cooking instructions as above.

Batinjan Gratin (Eggplants with White Sauce) is made with béchamel sauce instead of tomato sauce. To make the béchamel sauce, melt 4 tablespoons butter in a saucepan. Stir in 4 tablespoons flour and $\frac{1}{2}$ tablespoon salt. Add 2 cups of milk, all at once. Simmer over a medium flame while stirring the milk until thickened and bubbly. Cook and stir approximately 2 more minutes. Set aside.

Omit the tomato sauce and water from the recipe for Stuffed Eggplant Supreme and substitute the béchamel sauce to barely cover the eggplants. Bake at 350-375° until golden brown.

NOTE Serve with rice.

123

STUFFED ZUCCHINI
Kusa Mihshi

3 lbs. zucchini (12-14 zucchini up to 6 inches in length)
1 small chopped onion
1 T. butter
1 c. uncooked rice, long grain
1 lb. lamb shoulder, finely chopped
⅛ t. cinnamon
1 T. salt, plus 2 t.
pepper to taste
3 large tomatoes, peeled and diced, or 1-lb. can of stewed tomatoes

Core the zucchini, leaving ½-inch walls — be careful not to pierce the shell. Rinse the zucchini in cold water and drain. Sauté the onions in butter in a large pan. Rinse and drain the rice. Place it in a bowl. Add the meat, cinnamon, 1 tablespoon salt, and pepper; mix well. Then add half of the diced tomatoes to the meat and mix. Stuff the zucchini three-quarters full with the meat mixture or within an inch of the end (leave room for the rice to expand). Arrange the zucchini over the sautéed onions and pour the rest of the tomatoes on top. Barely cover with water and 2 teaspoons of additional salt.

Cover and cook on a medium flame for about 35 minutes or until the rice is done. Gently remove the zucchini to a serving platter. Serve the liquid in a pitcher. If desired, pour it over the zucchini and filling. Serve 1 to 3 zucchini per person.

6-8 SERVINGS

VARIATIONS

To make *Kusa bil-Laban* (Stuffed Zucchini in Yogurt), use the above recipe, excluding all of the tomatoes. Cook as instructed above. Drain the liquid. Add Yogurt Sauce (see page 190) for the last 10 minutes and simmer. To make *Batinjan Mihshi* (Stuffed Eggplants), substitute small eggplants (up to 5 inches in length) for the zucchini.

NOTE For a recipe using the cored portion of the zucchini, see *Mnazlit Kusa* (Zucchini Stew) — page 147.

STUFFED ZUCCHINI SUPREME
ʾAblama

¾ lb. lamb shoulder, coarsely ground
¼ t. cinnamon
salt and pepper to taste
½ c. pine nuts
1 large onion, finely chopped
10 small zucchini (5 inches in length)
1-3 T. butter
1 8-oz. can tomato sauce

Sauté the meat with the seasonings and pine nuts. Add the onions and continue sautéing until the onions are soft. Set aside.

Trim both ends of each zucchini and wash. Brown the zucchini in butter, turning frequently until they are slightly soft. Remove and place on a platter. Make a slit on the side of each zucchini. Stuff with 1-2 tablespoons of the filling. Arrange the zucchini next to each other in a pan. Pour the tomato sauce on top and barely cover with water. Sprinkle with additional salt. Bake in the oven at 375° for 25-30 minutes.

6 SERVINGS

NOTE This is usually served with rice.

STUFFED LAMB RIBS AND SOUP

Dil' Mihshi

FILLING

1 c. lamb, finely diced

½ c. uncooked rice

¼ c. pine nuts

⅛ t. cinnamon

⅛ t. allspice

salt and pepper to taste

1 large tomato, diced

SOUP

3-4 lbs. lamb ribs, cut with a pocket

1 T. salt

1 cinnamon stick

½ c. rice

1 small can tomato sauce or 2 tomatoes, diced

¼ c. parsley, chopped

Combine all the ingredients for the filling and loosely fill the pocketed ribs leaving room for the rice to expand. Skewer or sew the pockets and place them in a large pot or pressure cooker. Cover the meat with water, adding the salt and cinnamon stick. Cover and cook for half an hour. Add the rice and tomatoes, cooking until the rice is tender and the meat is done, approximately 25-30 minutes. Add the parsley and simmer 15 minutes more. Remove the ribs from the soup and place them on a platter to serve. Serve the soup for the first course, followed by the ribs.

4-6 SERVINGS

STUFFED CHICKEN AND SOUP
Djaj Mihshi

1 roasting chicken or large fryer
flour

STUFFING

1½ c. lamb, finely diced
½ c. uncooked rice
¼ c. butter, melted
⅛ t. cinnamon, plus for garnish
¼ t. allspice
salt and pepper to taste
¼ c. pine nuts

SOUP

1 T. salt
1 cinnamon stick
1 c. celery, diced
½ c. uncooked rice
¼ c. parsley, chopped

Clean the chicken by rubbing it with a small amount of flour on the outside and inside of the cavity. Rinse thoroughly with cold water. Mix all the stuffing ingredients and loosely stuff the chicken, leaving room for the rice to expand. Skewer or sew the opening shut. Place the chicken in a deep pot or pressure cooker. Completely cover the chicken with water, adding the salt and cinnamon stick. Bring to a boil, reduce the heat and simmer for an hour and a half or until the meat is tender (less if using a pressure cooker). The chicken is considered tender when the meat on the leg separates from the bone. Skim the *zafra* (fat curds) from the top of the chicken and the chicken stock when it appears. Add the celery and the rice during the last half hour of cooking. During the last 15 minutes add the parsley. Remove the chicken from the soup and place it on a platter to carve. Serve the soup for the first course, followed by the chicken. Sprinkle additional cinnamon on the carved chicken and stuffing.

4 SERVINGS

STUFFED TURKEY
Habash Mihshi

4 c. ground lamb or beef
½ c. butter, melted
6-8 c. cooked rice
½ c. pine nuts
½ c. blanched almonds, halved
2½ t. salt
1 t. allspice
1 t. pepper
½ t. cinnamon
½ c. water
12-14 lb. hen turkey

Sauté the ground meat until brown. Add the rest of the ingredients, except the water and the turkey, and continue sautéing for 5 minutes. Stuff the cavity of the turkey with the mixture. Sew or skewer the openings shut. Place the turkey in a roasting pan with the water and cover.

Bake at 450° for 1 hour. Lower to 325° and continue baking for 2 hours or until tender. Remove the cover for the last 15 minutes to brown.

8 SERVINGS

NOTE You can substitute 1½ c. chopped chestnuts for the pine nuts and almonds.

Stuffed Tripe and Casing Supreme

Ghammi

2 lbs. lamb or beef tripe and casings (they should come together from the butcher, but tripe alone can be used if casings are not available)

2 c. uncooked long grain rice

3 c. lamb shoulder, coarsely chopped

1 c. dried garbanzos, soaked overnight

2 large onions, coarsely chopped

½ t. saffron

1 t. cumin, plus ⅛ t.

½ t. allspice

½ t. cinnamon, plus ⅛ t.

½ t. pepper

1½ T. salt, plus 1 t

1 lemon, cut into wedges

Wash the tripe and casings well and let them drain. Cut the tripe into rectangles. (Finished, stuffed tripe is usually about 4-6 inches long by 2-4 inches but other shapes and sizes may be used to accommodate the original size of the tripe—the width is dependent upon whether it is beef or lamb tripe.) Fold the tripe rectangles in half and sew all but one edge.

Rinse the rice, drain, and add the rest of the ingredients, except ⅛ t. of cumin, ⅛ t. of cinnamon, 1 teaspoon of salt, and lemon wedges, to the rice. Mix well. Stuff the tripe two-thirds full with this mixture. Finish sewing the open side. Stuff the casings loosely with the aid of a funnel. Fit each casing over the small end of a funnel and fill with the tripe. Tie the ends of the casing with string.

Place the tripe and casings in a large pot and cover with water until it's 2 inches above the ghammi. Add an additional ⅛ teaspoon of cinnamon, cumin, and 1 teaspoon of salt to the water. Boil until the tripe is done—when a fork will pierce it easily. More water may need to be added during cooking. Remove the fat curds as they form on top of the broth.

RECIPE CONTINUES >

Remove the stuffed ghammi from the broth. Remove the thread. Cut the tripe into bite-size pieces and toss with the filling. Cut the casings into desired lengths and serve around the tripe and filling. Garnish with lemon wedges. The broth may be used as a hot appetizer or as a first course.

6-8 SERVINGS

NOTE When cooking *Ghammi* in the Middle East, it also includes the head and hooves of the lamb. *Ghammi* is always considered a treat as well as a delicacy for it takes much preparation and time.

130

STUFFED POTATOES
Mihshi Batata

8 medium potatoes (about 4 inches in length)
¼ c. pine nuts
½ c. butter
1 lb. lamb shoulder, finely chopped
1 large onion, finely chopped
⅛ t. cinnamon
salt and pepper to taste
1 can tomato sauce or 2 large fresh tomatoes, diced

Peel the potatoes; hollow a pocket in each potato leaving ½-inch walls and a 1-inch opening. Do not pierce the opposite end. Place the potatoes in cold water until ready for use.

Sauté the pine nuts in butter until golden brown. Add the meat and sauté for about 10 minutes. Add the onions and seasonings and cook for a few minutes more. Stuff the potatoes with the meat mixture and arrange the potatoes upright in a baking dish. Pour the tomato sauce, or diced tomatoes, on top of the potatoes. Barely cover with water. Cover and bake in a 400° oven for 30-45 minutes or until done.

6-8 SERVINGS

131

NOTE The potatoes may also be arranged upright in a pan and cooked on top of the stove on medium heat, 25-30 minutes. In Lebanon this is usually served with rice.

RICE DISHES
اطباق الارز

ARABIC PLAIN RICE
Riz Mfalfal

RICE WITH VERMICELLI
Riz bish-Sh'iriyyi

CAULIFLOWER WITH RICE
Yakhnit al-Qarnabit

SPINACH WITH RICE
Sbanikh bir-Riz

RICE WITH FAVA BEANS
Ful maʿ ar-Riz

RICE WITH CHICKEN GIBLETS
Riz Maʿ Hwahis ad-Djaj

RICE WITH MEAT
Riz Tajin

UPSIDE DOWN RICE
Riz bid-Dfin

RICE TO THE MIDDLE EASTERNER is what potatoes are to the Irish. Rice is often cooked with vegetables. These combination dishes are usually layered. First the meat is sautéed, then vegetables and rice are added. Then the three layers are inverted onto a serving plate so that the meat is on the top.

The main points to remember when cooking with rice are use long grain rice; salt the water well to yield fluffy separated rice kernels; and do not stir the rice once the water has evaporated.

ARABIC PLAIN RICE
Riz Mfalfal

¼ c. butter
1 c. uncooked rice, long grain
2 c. water
1 T. salt

Melt the butter in a saucepan. Rinse the rice in cold water, drain, and add to the butter. Sauté for a few minutes. Add the water and salt. Cover, bring to a boil, and cook for about 5 minutes. Lower the heat and simmer for 15 minutes. The rice is done when all the water is absorbed and the kernels are flaky.

4 SERVINGS

134

RICE WITH VERMICELLI
Riz bish-Sh'iriyyi

½ c. vermicelli, about ½ doz. pieces cut into 1-2-inch lengths
¼ c. butter
1 c. uncooked rice, long grain
2½ c. water
1 T. salt

Brown the vermicelli in the butter. Rinse the rice in cold water, drain, and sauté with the vermicelli for a few minutes. Add the water and salt, cover, and cook for 20 minutes on medium heat, then simmer for 5 minutes. When done, the rice and vermicelli should be tender.

4 SERVINGS

CAULIFLOWER WITH RICE
Yakhnit al-Qarnabit

1 lb. lamb shoulder, finely chopped or ground
1 small onion, chopped
1 medium head of cauliflower, cut into florets
2½-3 c. water
1 c. uncooked rice, long grain
⅛ t. cinnamon
salt and pepper to taste

Sauté the meat. Add the onions and continue sautéing until the onions are limp. Add the cauliflower and water (the water should barely cover the cauliflower). Bring to a boil, add the rice and seasonings, and lower to medium heat. Cover. Cook until the rice is tender, about 20 minutes. Let stand for a few minutes. Turn the pan upside down onto a platter to unmold.

4-6 SERVINGS

SPINACH WITH RICE
Sbanikh bir-Riz

1 medium onion, chopped
2 T. oil or butter
1 bunch of fresh spinach
2⅓ c. water
salt and pepper to taste
1 c. uncooked rice, long grain
lemon wedges, garnish

Sauté the onions with seasonings in the oil until lightly brown.

Wash the spinach and cut coarsely (each leaf in about 3 pieces). Add the spinach to the onions, cover, and cook until the spinach is slightly limp. Add the water, salt and pepper, and rice. Do not stir. Cook for 10 minutes on medium high heat or until it comes to a boil. Then lower the heat and simmer for 15 minutes. To serve, place a platter on top of the pan and turn it upside down. Let it stand a few minutes to settle. Garnish with lemon.

4 SERVINGS

137

NOTE To add a layer of meat, sauté ½ pound of ground beef with the onions. Add the coarsely cut spinach and proceed as above.

RICE WITH FAVA BEANS

Ful ma(ar-Riz

1 lb. lamb shoulder, cut into 1-inch squares
½ c. butter
1 medium onion, chopped
⅛ t. allspice
salt and pepper to taste
1 lb. young fresh fava beans
4½ c. hot water
2 c. uncooked long grain rice

In a pan, brown the meat in the butter until the redness is gone, stirring constantly. Add the onions and seasonings and continue sautéing. Shell the fava beans; cut the pods into thirds and add to the meat. Cover and let steam for 10 minutes. Add the hot water and bring the mixture to a boil. Add the rice. Simmer for about 30 minutes or until the rice is done and the water has evaporated.

138

    To serve, place a platter on the pot, invert the pot onto the plate and let it stand for a few minutes before removing.

6 SERVINGS

RICE WITH
CHICKEN GIBLETS
Riz Ma⁽ Hwabis ad-Djaj

¼ lb. giblets
2 c. uncooked rice, long grain
1 small onion, chopped, optional
½ c. butter
4½ c. chicken broth, or water may be substituted for part of the broth
1 t. allspice
¼ t. cinnamon, plus cinnamon to garnish
1-2 t. salt
½ c. almond halves or chopped walnuts
½ c. seedless raisins
¼ c. pine nuts, browned in butter, optional

Completely cover the giblets with water and boil until tender. Remove the fat curds as they form. Remove the giblets and reserve the broth. Cut the giblets into small pieces and set aside. Meanwhile, rinse the rice in cold water and drain.

In a large pan, sauté the onions in butter until limp. Add the rice and continue sautéing for a few minutes. Measure the giblet broth and add enough chicken broth to equal 4½ cups. Add the seasonings and rice mixture. The giblets mixture should taste salty; adjust accordingly. Cover. Bring to a boil and cook for 20 minutes on a medium flame. Add the almonds, or chopped walnuts, raisins, and giblets. Stir gently with a fork. Simmer for 10 additional minutes.

Pour onto a flat platter, heaping the rice in the center. Sprinkle with cinnamon and the browned pine nuts, if desired.

8 SERVINGS

NOTE This is excellent for buffets or parties. If white rice is preferred, omit the allspice and cinnamon. Turkey giblets may be substituted. The top may be garnished with sliced pieces of chicken, then sprinkled with cinnamon.

139

RICE WITH MEAT
Riz Tajin

1½ lbs. lamb, diced
1 large onion, coarsely chopped
¼ t. cinnamon
salt and pepper to taste
½ c. butter
½ c. pine nuts
2 c. uncooked rice, long grain
4 c. boiling water
grated cheese

Sauté the meat, onions, and seasonings in the butter until most of the pink is gone from the meat ad the onions are translucent but not limp. Add the pine nuts and continue sautéing for 5 minutes. Place the meat mixture in an even layer in a casserole dish or a glass or earthenware baking dish. Add the rice and cover with the boiling water. Top with grated cheese. Cover and bake at 325° for 1 hour or until the rice is tender.

Remove and run a knife around edge of the pan. Turn it upside down onto a serving dish. Let it stand for few minutes before removing the casserole dish.

6-8 SERVINGS

UPSIDE DOWN RICE
Riz bid-Dfin

4 lamb shanks, or beef
1 large onion, quartered and sliced
2½ c. broth
½ c. butter
⅛ t. allspice
⅛ t. cinnamon
salt and pepper to taste
1 15½-oz. can garbanzo beans, drained
1 c. uncooked rice, long grain

Cover the shanks and onions with cold water and cook for about 2 hours or until tender. Remove the *zafra*, or fat curds, as they form. Debone and shred the meat.

Place the meat back in the pot with the broth, onions, butter, and seasonings. Add the garbanzo beans and rice. Add salt if needed. Cook for 20-25 minutes on a medium flame until the rice is done and the water is evaporated. Do not stir. Turn the heat off and let stand for 5 minutes.

Turn the pot upside down on a serving platter and let stand for a few minutes before unmolding.

4-6 SERVINGS

141

LENTEN (VEGETARIAN) DISHES
اطباق بدون لحوم

EGGPLANT APPETIZER
Baba Ghannuj

EGGPLANT AND GARBANZO STEW
Mnazlit Batinjan

ZUCCHINI STEW
Mnazlit Kusa

SPIRIT OF THE COOK
Tabbakh Ruhu

SAUTÉED DANDELION GREENS
Hindbi Miqliyyi

GARBANZO BEAN DIP
Hummus bit-Tahini

GREEN BEAN STEW
Lubyi biz-Zayt

OKRA WITH OIL
Bamyi biz-Zayt

FRIED VEGETABLES
Khudar Miqliyyi

GREEN FAVA BEANS
Ful biz-Zayt

FAVA BEAN POTTAGE
Ful Imdammas

FAVA BEAN PATTIES
Falafel

EGG OMELET
Ijji

CAULIFLOWER OMELET
Ijjit Qarnabit

EGGS WITH TOMATOES
Bayd biI-Banadura

LENTIL POTTAGE
Mjadra

LENTILS WITH RICE
Mdardra

LENTILS WITH CRUSHED WHEAT
Mjadra biI-Burghul

LENTEN STUFFED GRAPE LEAVES
Mihshi Waraq 'Inab Siyami

STUFFED SWISS CHARD
Mihshi Waraq Silq

STUFFED CABBAGE LEAVES IN OIL
Mihshi Malfuf biz-Zayt

MACARONI WITH MILK
Ma'karuni biI-Halib

MACARONI WITH TOMATO SAUCE
Ma'karuni biz-Zayt

MACARONI WITH TAHINI SAUCE
Ma'karuni bit-Taratur

WHOLE WHEAT FOR MEMORIAL SERVICES
Sayniyyat an-Niyaha

THERE ARE MANY RELIGIOUS HOLIDAYS, both in the Eastern and the Western churches, that have periods of fasting. Lenten fasting is an integral and important part of the daily lives of the people of the Middle East.

The Eastern Orthodox Church has the following Lenten periods: the Great Lent, 40 days prior to Easter; the Dormition Feast, or the falling asleep of the Blessed Virgin, 15 days; the Christmas Fast, 40 days before Christmas; the Feast of the Holy Apostles, 1 day; the day before Epiphany; the Feast of the Beheading of St. John the Baptist; the Feast of the Elevation of the Holy Cross; and every Wednesday and Friday, with few exceptions during the year. The types of food that can be eaten during these Lenten periods vary. For example, during the Great Lent, there is a gradual withdrawal from meat, to dairy products, to a vegan diet.

The meatless recipes in this section and throughout the book are only a sampling of the foods that are a part of the rich Middle Eastern religious heritage. Of course, these dishes may be used any time of the year as well as on special occasions.

HINTS

~ When dicing, chopping, or frying eggplant, always place them in salted cold water so they won't turn dark; eggplant will also take less oil than other vegetables when frying.

~ Meatless dishes may be eaten hot or cold.

~ When using lemon juice in the recipes, personal preference, desired tartness, will dictate the quantity.

Eggplant Appetizer
Baba Ghannuj

1 large eggplant
1 clove garlic
salt to taste
4 T. *tahini*
¼ c. water
¼-½ c. lemon juice, depending upon desired tartness
finely chopped parsley and/or pomegranate seeds, garnish

Bake or grill the eggplant until well done. Alternatively, char the eggplant over the open flame of a gas burner, turning frequently. Place the eggplant in a bowl and remove the skin carefully, reserving the liquid. Chop finely.

In the bowl of a food processor, combine the garlic with the salt. Add the *tahini* and blend thoroughly; slowly add the water, mixing well. Add lemon juice and thoroughly blend. Add the eggplant and pulse 2 or 3 times. Garnish the edge of the serving dish with parsley, placing a small mound in the center; or, garnish with pomegranate seeds and chopped parsley.

4-6 SERVINGS

NOTE This may be used as an appetizer or a side dish for Lenten season. Arabic custom is to pour a small amount of olive oil over the top as well as a sprinkling of *simmaq*.

EGGPLANT AND GARBANZO STEW
Mnazlit Batinjan

1 large eggplant
1 large onion, chopped
½ c. olive oil
1 15½-oz. can garbanzo beans, drained
salt and pepper to taste
3 fresh tomatoes, or 1 can whole tomatoes, or 1 small can of tomato sauce

Peel the eggplant and cut it into 3-inch wedges. Sauté the onions in the olive oil in a saucepan. Add the garbanzo beans and eggplant. Add the seasonings. Cover and simmer for 15 minutes. (Gently rotate the vegetables a couple of times during cooking by holding the lid tightly on the pan and tossing.) Then add the tomatoes and a little water if you're using fresh tomatoes. (The liquid should come to half the depth of the vegetables in the pan.) Cook on a medium flame until the eggplant is done, about 20-25 minutes. Serve hot or cold.

4-6 SERVINGS

ZUCCHINI STEW

Mnazlit Kusa

1 medium onion, chopped
½ c. olive oil
1 or 2 large zucchini, finely chopped
3 fresh tomatoes, diced, or 1 can whole tomatoes
salt and pepper to taste
2 eggs, lightly beaten

Sauté the onions in oil in a saucepan. Add the zucchini, tomatoes, and seasonings. Simmer for 15 minutes or until tender. Add the eggs and stir thoroughly, for a couple of minutes; until the eggs are set.

4 SERVINGS

NOTE Both the eggs and the tomatoes are optional.

147

SPIRIT OF THE COOK
Tabbakh Ruhu

1-lb. zucchini
2 large cloves garlic
1 T. dry or 2 T. fresh mint
salt to taste
¼ c. olive oil
pepper to taste

Wash and halve or quarter the zucchini, depending on the size. If too thick, cut in half. Mash the garlic, mint, and salt together. Layer the garlic mixture with the zucchini in a deep pan. The top layer should be the garlic mixture. Pour the oil over the top layer and season with a little pepper. Cook on medium heat for 20-25 minutes or until the zucchini is tender.

4-6 SERVINGS

SAUTÉED DANDELION GREENS
Hindbi Miqliyyi

2 bunches of dandelion greens
2 medium onions, julienned
1 clove garlic, chopped, optional
2 T. olive oil
salt to taste
1 T. water
lemon wedges

Thoroughly clean the greens and cook until they are wilted but not soft, about 5 minutes. Drain, squeezing out the excess moisture, then coarsely chop.

Sauté the onions and garlic in the oil until golden brown. Reserve two-thirds of the onions for the top and mix the rest with the greens. Add the salt and water; cover and simmer for 10 minutes. Spread the greens on a platter and cover the entire top with the reserved onions. Serve with lemon, which may be squeezed on top before serving or in wedges for individual taste.

4-6 SERVINGS

149

GARBANZO BEAN DIP
Hummus bit-Tahini

1 15½-oz. can garbanzo beans, drained
3 T. *tahini*
¼-½ c. lemon juice
1 clove garlic
⅛ t. cumin
½ t. salt
finely chopped parsley and/or pomegranate seeds, garnish
olive oil, optional
simmaq, optional

Process all of the ingredients, except for 1 tablespoon of the garbanzos, the parsley, olive oil, and *simmaq*, in a food processor and add water to just below the level of the garbanzos. Process, adding additional water as necessary, to form a smooth, thick paste. Garnish the edge of a serving dish with the parsley. Place the hummus in the middle of the dish. Mound the reserved garbanzo beans in the center of the hummus with a few leaves of parsley. Arabic custom is to pour a small amount of olive oil over the top as well as a sprinkling of *simmaq*.

4 SERVINGS

NOTE This may be used as an appetizer or as a side dish for a main meal. Serve with Arabic Bread (see page 12).

150

GREEN BEAN STEW
Lubyi biz-Zayt

1 lb. fresh green beans, or frozen
1 large clove garlic, chopped
1 medium onion, chopped
¼ c. olive oil
salt and pepper to taste
½ c. water
1 8-oz. can tomato sauce

Snip the ends off the beans. Wash and cut into 2-inch lengths.

Sauté the garlic and onion in olive oil. Add the seasonings. Add the beans to the onion mixture, tossing lightly. Cover and steam for 10 minutes, tossing once during the cooking process. Add the water and tomato sauce.

Cover and cook 20-25 minutes.

4-6 SERVINGS

NOTE The beans can be served as a side dish or with rice.

151

OKRA WITH OIL
Bamyi biz-Zayt

1 lb. young whole okra
⅔ c. olive oil
1 medium onion, chopped
3 cloves garlic, chopped
2 t. coriander seed or ½ t. ground coriander
salt and pepper to taste
1 8-oz. can tomato sauce
½-¾ c. lemon juice

Clean the okra with a slightly dampened cloth. Cut off the stems. Sauté in the olive oil until lightly brown. Remove okra and set aside.

Place the oil remaining from the okra in a saucepan and sauté the onions, garlic, and seasonings. Add the okra to the sautéed onions, then add the tomato sauce and enough water to barely cover the okra. Cook on a medium flame for 20-25 minutes. Add the lemon juice to the okra and simmer for 10 minutes.

4 SERVINGS

NOTE This is especially good served over plain fluffy rice or vermicelli rice. Frozen okra may be used. If so, no need to sauté the okra.

FRIED VEGETABLES
Khudar Miqliyyi

$\frac{1}{2}$ head cauliflower
1 large or 2 medium zucchini
1 medium eggplant, peeled lengthwise, leaving 1-inch strips of skin intact
1 large potato, peeled
2-3 T. olive oil
2 medium tomatoes
fresh mint, garnish
salt

Cut the cauliflower into small florets. Cut the zucchini and eggplant into $\frac{1}{2}$-inch rounds and the potato into $\frac{1}{4}$-inch rounds. Soak the eggplant in salt water for about 15 minutes and drain well before frying.

Heat the oil until it's hot. Fry the potatoes until tender and golden brown. Remove them from the frying pan and drain. Continue frying the rest of the vegetables until tender and golden brown. Slice the tomatoes and fry just before serving.

153

Arrange the vegetables in rows on a platter and garnish with sprigs of fresh mint. Salt the entire platter just before serving. Serve hot or cold.

4 SERVINGS

NOTE This is often served for summer meals or during Lenten season and is especially good accompanied with Cucumber-Yogurt Salad (see page 177) and Arabic Bread (see page 12).

GREEN FAVA BEANS
Ful biz-Zayt

2 lbs. fresh and tender fava beans
3 cloves garlic
1 medium onion, chopped
salt and pepper to taste
$\frac{1}{8}$ t. allspice
$\frac{1}{2}$ c. olive oil
1 t. coriander seed
$\frac{1}{2}$-1 c. water
$\frac{1}{3}$ c. lemon juice

Wash and shell the fava beans. Remove the string from the edges of the pods and discard. Cut the pods into 1-inch lengths. Place the beans and pods in cold water so they will not discolor.

154

Chop 2 cloves of the garlic. Sauté the onions, chopped garlic, salt, pepper, and allspice in the oil until it's lightly browned. Mash the remaining clove of garlic with the coriander seed and add to the onion mixture; sauté for a few more minutes. Add the drained beans and pods, tossing thoroughly. Add the water and cook on a medium flame for 20-25 minutes or until the beans and pods are almost tender. Add the lemon juice and simmer for 5 minutes.

6-8 SERVINGS

NOTE Serve with rice.

Fava Bean Pottage

Ful Imdammas

2 c. dried fava beans
1 clove garlic
½ t. salt
½ c. lemon juice
1 small onion, finely chopped
¼ c. olive oil
½ c. parsley, finely chopped, garnish
green onions, garnish
lemon wedges, garnish

Soak the fava beans overnight in cold water. Drain, cover with fresh water, and cook on a low flame until tender. (It takes at least an hour.) Add water, if necessary, to prevent sticking and to keep the mixture soupy.

In a large bowl, mash the garlic with the salt. Add the lemon juice, mixing well. Add the onions, beans and liquid, and olive oil. Mix thoroughly. Garnish with chopped parsley and serve with green onions and lemon wedges. May be served hot or cold.

4-6 SERVINGS

NOTE Arabic Bread (see page 12) works well with this.

Fava Bean Patties
Falafel

1 lb. dried fava beans
1 small onion, coarsely chopped
2 cloves garlic, crushed
1 t. ground coriander
¼ t. hot (red) pepper, optional
1 t. soda
½ t. cumin
salt and pepper to taste
1 T. flour
½ c. oil

156

Soak the fava beans in cold water for 3-4 days, changing the water every day. Peel the beans and place them with the onion in the bowl of a food processor. Add the rest of the ingredients, except the oil. Mix well. Process the mixture a second time. Form the mixture into 2-2½-inch patties and deep fry or pan fry in hot oil.

6-8 SERVINGS

NOTE *Falafel* patties are delightful in sandwiches with Arabic Bread (see page 12), or as hors d'oeuvres (make walnut-sized balls and deep fry). If you'd prefer a mixture of beans, soak ¾ cup of garbanzo beans with the fava beans. Then follow the instructions above.

EGG OMELET
Ijji

4 eggs
½ c. milk
⅛ t. cinnamon
salt and pepper to taste
1 small onion, finely chopped
½ c. parsley, finely chopped
2 small green onions, finely chopped
¼ c. chopped green mint, optional
4 T. oil

Beat the eggs. Add the milk and continue beating. Mix the seasonings with the onions and work together with your fingers. Add to the eggs along with the parsley, green onions, and mint. Mix well.

157

Oil a 7- or 8-inch square pan and heat it in the oven. Pour the mixture into the hot pan and bake at 400° until done, approximately 15 minutes. Check the omelet with a toothpick to determine it's cooked through. Cut in squares and serve.

4-6 SERVINGS

NOTE This may be prepared on top of the stove too. Flip the omelet once during cooking.

CAULIFLOWER OMELET
Ijjit Qarnabit

4 eggs
1 c. milk
⅛ t. cinnamon
salt and pepper to taste
2 c. finely grated cauliflower
⅓ c. finely chopped onion
3 green onions, with stems, chopped
½ c. parsley
⅓ c. butter

Beat the eggs and milk thoroughly. Add the seasonings, cauliflower, onions and green onions, and parsley. Mix well.

Melt the butter in a 7- or 8-inch square pan in the oven. Pour the egg mixture in the hot pan and bake at 350° for about 15-20 minutes or until it is firm. Cut in squares.

4-6 SERVINGS

Eggs with Tomatoes

Bayd bil-Banadura

2 medium ripe tomatoes
1 T. butter or olive oil
4 eggs
$\frac{1}{8}$ t. cinnamon
salt and pepper

Peel and dice the tomatoes. Melt the butter or olive oil in a skillet. Add the tomatoes and simmer for a few minutes. Meanwhile beat the eggs well; add the seasonings. Pour the eggs over the tomatoes and mix gently. Cover and cook over low heat
for about 10 minutes or until done.

4-6 SERVINGS

NOTE Another variation would be to begin with a large, diced potato (cooked or
raw). Fry the potato until lightly browned then add the tomatoes. Proceed as above.

159

LENTIL POTTAGE
Mjadra

1 c. dried lentils
4 c. water
1 large onion, chopped
2 T. olive oil
⅛ t. pepper
⅛ t. cumin, optional
salt to taste
½ c. uncooked rice

Rinse the lentils and place them in a pot with the water. Boil for 20 minutes on a medium flame. Sauté the onions in the oil, then add the onions and residue, seasonings, and rice to the lentils. Cover and cook for 20 minutes. Stir occasionally. Serve on a platter—this thickens as it cools. Serve hot or room temperature.

4-6 SERVINGS

NOTE This differs from *Mdardra* (Lentils with Rice) in that *Mjadra* (Lentil Pottage) is always moist while *Mdardra* is always dry and flaky.

LENTILS WITH RICE

Mðarðra

1 c. uncooked lentils
4 c. water
2 large red onions, julienned
½ c. olive oil
1 c. uncooked rice
1 T. salt

Rinse the lentils and add them to the water. Bring to a boil and cook over medium heat for 15 minutes.

Meanwhile sauté the onions in oil until golden brown. Remove the onions from the pan and rinse the frying pan with 2 tablespoons of lentil water. Reserve the onions. Add this residue, the rice, and salt to the lentils. Cook for 20-25 minutes or until the rice and lentils are fluffy.

Place the *Mðarðra* on a serving platter and completely cover it with the fried onions. Serve hot or room temperature.

6 SERVINGS

LENTILS WITH CRUSHED WHEAT
Mjadra bil-Burghul

1 c. dried lentils
5 c. water
1 large onion, chopped
½ c. olive oil
⅛ t. pepper
⅔ t. salt
⅓ c. *burghul*, #3

Rinse the lentils and place them in a pan with the water. Cover and bring to a boil; continue boiling for 15 minutes on medium heat. Sauté the onions in the oil. Add the onions and residue, seasonings, and *burghul* to the lentils. Cover and cook for an additional 25 minutes, stirring occasionally.

Serve in a bowl, or on a platter. This thickens as it cools and may be eaten hot or cold.

4-6 SERVINGS

LENTEN STUFFED GRAPE LEAVES
Mihshi Waraq 'Inab Siyami

1½ c. parsley
2 large tomatoes, peeled
½ bunch of green onions
1 small onion
1 c. uncooked rice
½ c. lemon juice
½ c. olive oil
40-50 grape leaves (3-4 inches), fresh or canned
1 T. salt

Finely chop all of the vegetables, except the grape leaves, and mix well. Rinse the rice in cold water and drain. Add the rice, lemon juice, and oil to the vegetables. Mix well.

Place a bowl of hot water near your work area. Wilt the grape leaves by rinsing them a few times in the hot water. Drain. Place a heaping teaspoon of the filling on the edge of the dull side of a leaf. Begin rolling as with a jelly roll. After the first roll, fold in the ends and continue rolling. The rolled grape leaf should be about ½-¾-inches thick, depending on the size of the leaf.

Place a few leaves in the bottom of a 2½-quart pan to prevent sticking. Arrange the rolls in compact rows and barely cover them with water. Sprinkle a tablespoonful of salt on top of the rolls and place a pottery plate over them so the rolls will remain firm and intact. Cover the pan and cook on a medium flame for 15 minutes. Lower the heat and simmer for an additional 15 minutes. Unmold by placing the plate over the pan and inverting. If any rolls fall out of place, reinsert them.

8 SERVINGS

NOTE See page 118 for a diagram of Stuffed Grape Leaves.

Stuffed Swiss Chard
Mihshi Waraq Silq

1 lb. Swiss chard
1 15½-oz. can garbanzo beans, drained
1 c. parsley, finely chopped
1 bunch of green onions, chopped
1 c. uncooked rice
½ c. lemon juice, plus 2-3 T.
½ c. olive oil
salt and pepper to taste, plus 1 T. salt

Clean the Swiss chard and wilt it by dipping the leaves in hot water for a second. Slice each leaf in half on the rib. If the rib is thick, remove excess. The leaves should be roughly 6 inches long and 4 inches wide. (However, they can vary.) Set aside 3 or 4 leaves of Swiss chard.

Mix all of the remaining ingredients, except 2-3 teaspoons of lemon juice and 1 tablespoon of salt. Place 1 tablespoon of the filling on each leaf, spreading the filling lengthwise. Roll as for a jelly roll, folding in both ends after the first roll to secure the filling. (The ends may be left open and the roll given a squeeze before placing in a medium-sized pot or Dutch oven.) The diameter of the roll should be no more than ¾-inch thick. Reserve any liquid left from the filling.

Remove the ribs from the reserved leaves. Layer them on the bottom of the pot. Arrange the stuffed Swiss chard in compact rows over the layer of ribs. (When arranging the rows, work from the outside towards the center, filling empty spaces with smaller rolls. Alternate the direction of the rolls every other row.) Barely cover the rolls with water and the remaining liquid from the filling. Sprinkle 1 tablespoon of salt over the top. Place a heat-proof pottery plate over the rolls so that they will remain firm and intact. Cover the pot and cook on a medium flame 15 minutes. Add an additional 2 or 3 tablespoons of lemon juice and cook for 10 minutes more. Serve hot or cold.

When serving, if there is excess liquid, drain. Unmold by placing a plate over the pan and inverting. If any rolls fall out, reinsert them.

6-8 SERVINGS

STUFFED CABBAGE LEAVES IN OIL
Mibshi Malfuf biz-Zayt

1 large head of white cabbage
1 c. uncooked rice, long grain
1 small onion, finely chopped
½ bunch green onions, finely chopped
1 c. parsley, finely chopped
1 c. olive oil
salt and pepper to taste, plus 1 t. salt
2 large tomatoes, finely chopped
3 cloves garlic, plus 1 clove
¼ c. dry mint or ½ c. fresh mint, finely chopped
¼ c. lemon juice

Core the cabbage and parboil the head in a large kettle of water just long enough to soften and separate the leaves. Break off the leaves and set them aside to drain. If any cabbage veins are excessively thick, reduce them with a sharp knife. Cover the bottom of a medium sized pot or Dutch oven with the cut-away portion of the cabbage leaves. Cut the large leaves in half along the center vein.

Thoroughly mix the rest of the ingredients with the exception of 1 teaspoon of salt, the garlic, the mint, and lemon juice. Place a generous tablespoon of the mixture on the thicker edge of each leaf. Roll as in a jelly roll. Squeeze the rolls gently when placing them compactly in the pot. Chop 3 cloves of the garlic. Sprinkle the garlic between each layer. The number of layers will depend on the size of the pot.

Mash together the mint, 1 clove of garlic, and 1 teaspoon of salt. Stir in the lemon juice and pour the mixture over the rolled cabbage leaves. Add enough water to cover the rolls. Place a small oven-proof dish on top of the leaves to keep them from separating. Cover and cook on a medium flame 20-25 minutes, then simmer on a low flame for 15 minutes or until the rice is tender.

8 SERVINGS

MACARONI WITH MILK
Maʿkaruni bil-Halib

1 lb. spaghetti
1 T. butter
4 eggs, well beaten
4 c. milk
1½ t. salt
2 T. fresh parsley, finely chopped or 2 t. dried parsley
½ c. grated Gruyere or Parmesan cheese

Cook the spaghetti in salted boiling water. Rinse in cold water and place in a buttered 9 x 13-inch pan.

Thoroughly mix the eggs, milk, salt, and parsley with a fork. Pour it over the spaghetti. Top with grated cheese. Bake at 350° for 25-35 minutes or until the mixture sets.

6-8 SERVINGS

MACARONI
WITH TOMATO SAUCE
Ma'karuni biz-Zayt

2 c. elbow macaroni

1 medium onion, chopped

2 T. olive oil

2 large cloves garlic

1 t. sweet basil

1 t. salt, plus salt and pepper to taste

1 8-oz. can tomato sauce

$\frac{1}{8}$ t. cinnamon

Boil the macaroni in salted water until done, about 10 minutes. Drain and rinse in cold water. In a sauce pan, sauté the onions in oil until golden. Mash the garlic and sweet basil with 1 teaspoon salt. Add this mixture to the onion and continue sautéing for another minute. Add the tomato sauce, cinnamon, and salt and pepper to taste. Bring the sauce to a boil, add the macaroni and heat through. Serve hot.

4-6 SERVINGS

MACARONI WITH TAHINI SAUCE
Ma'karuni bit-Taratur

2 c. elbow macaroni or ¼ lb. spaghetti
1 large clove garlic
¼ t. salt, plus salt and pepper to taste
3 T. *tahini*
3 T. water
3 T. lemon juice
2 T. parsley, coarsely chopped

Cook the macaroni or spaghetti in salted boiling water. Mash the garlic and salt in a large bowl. Add the *tahini*, mixing well. Gradually add the water, blending thoroughly, then add the lemon juice. Blend well. When the macaroni is cooked, drain and rinse it in cold water. Add the parsley and macaroni to the *tahini* sauce and toss thoroughly. Add salt and pepper to taste. Serve hot or cold.

4-6 SERVINGS

WHOLE WHEAT FOR MEMORIAL SERVICES

Sayniyyat an-Niyaha

4 lbs. whole wheat kernels

1 T. anise seed

1 lb. garbanzo beans, unsalted and roasted

silver doilies

1 lb. powdered sugar

1 lb. sugar-coated almonds, white

silver décors

Combine the whole wheat and anise seed and completely cover with water. Cook about an hour and a half, until tender. The kernels should not be opened. Drain thoroughly. Spread on a towel until the kernels are dry but tender (6-8 hours).

Process the unsalted and roasted garbanzo beans in the bowl of a food processor until powdery. Sift to remove the large chunks. On a 15 x 22-inch silver tray, cut the silver doilies in half and arrange them around the outside edge of the tray; tape them down. Place rectangular wax paper on the tray overlapping the doilies approximately 1 inch, forming a scalloped design. Spread ⅓ of the whole wheat evenly on the wax paper; gently press down using a piece of wax paper between your hand and the whole wheat. Repeat until all of the whole wheat is used; the rectangle will be compact and slightly rounded on the sides. Sift the powdered garbanzo beans evenly on top of the whole wheat to generously cover; press down with the waxed paper. The wheat should not show.

About 2 hours before serving, sift powdered sugar on top covering the powdered garbanzo beans thoroughly. Press down with waxed paper, especially around the edges. Arrange the sugar-coated almonds around the edge of the tray. Make a cross with the silver décors in the center. Using tweezers, press each décors slightly into the sugar in order to hold it. On either side of the cross, place the first and last initial of the deceased with the silver décors.

3 DOZEN

NOTE This may be offered in memory of departed persons for the 40 day memorial service, and again at intervals of 3, 6, and 12 months.

169

LABAN (YOGURT) DISHES
اطباق اللبن

YOGURT
Laban

ARABIC CHEESE
Jibin

CHEESE PASTE
Labni

CHEESE FILLED OMELET
'Ijji bil-Labni

PRESERVED YOGURT
CHEESE BALLS
Labni Makbusi

CUCUMBER-YOGURT
SALAD
Khyar bil-Laban

EGGS IN MINT
YOGURT SAUCE
Laban bil-Bayd

LAMB SUPREME
WITH YOGURT
Laban 'Ummu

STUFFED LAMB
DELICACIES
IN YOGURT SAUCE
Shishbarak

EGGPLANT WITH YOGURT
Batinjan bil-Laban

GARBANZO BEANS
WITH ARABIC CROUTONS
Fatti bil-Hummus

LAMB SHANKS
WITH ARABIC CROUTONS
Fatti Mqadim al-Ghanam

RAWBI IS THE STARTER CULTURE used for making *laban*, or yogurt. In the Middle East, no home is without *laban*, which is made from goat or cow milk. *Laban* and its derivatives are to the Middle East as milk and cream sauces are to the Western cultures and diets. In Lebanon *laban* is never served with fish.

Laban can be made from skim or whole milk, depending on the preference of the cook. However, for recipes using *laban* as its base, it is best to use whole milk.

YOGURT
Laban

½ gallon whole milk
2 T. *rawbi*, or a starter can be taken from commercial plain yogurt

Pour the milk in a heavy pan and heat on a low flame until it comes to a boil. Remove from the flame. Pour the milk into a serving bowl or jar. Cool to 115° (or when the little finger can be immersed in the milk to the count of ten).

Using a paper towel, absorb the separated liquid standing on the starter. Stir the starter until it's smooth. Remove the scum from the heated milk. Add the scum plus one additional tablespoon of warm milk to the starter. Blend well. Add the starter mixture to the warm milk and stir.

Cover the bowl with a plate. Place heavy towels completely around the bowl to retain the heat. Let stand in a warm place overnight or for 8 hours. *Laban* should not be disturbed during this time. Refrigerate for a couple of hours before using.

8 SERVINGS

173

NOTE Always save 2 tablespoons of yogurt, before using, and place in a covered jar as a *rawbi* for the next recipe. If the *rawbi* is from commercial yogurt, the results will be sweeter than a *rawbi* from yogurt made at home. If the yogurt does not congeal, warm the covered bowl over hot water (not boiling) for 45-60 minutes.

ARABIC CHEESE
Jibin

1 gallon whole milk
1 Hansen's Cheese Rennet or 1 junket tablet
2 T. cold water
salt

Heat the milk to lukewarm in a heavy pan over a low flame. Remove from the heat and keep warm. Dissolve the tablet in the water. Add it to the milk and stir. Cover and let stand for 45 minutes or until it thickens. (The cheese is ready when a watery substance appears when cutting into the curd.)

Pour the mixture into a cheesecloth-lined colander and let stand until most of the whey has drained away. Then pour it into a 2½-inch-thick round or square pan. Place plastic wrap on top and refrigerate. Drain the water from the pan every day for 2 days. On the third day, sprinkle the mixture with salt, turn it over into another pan, and sprinkle it again; then place it back in the original pan. In a week the cheese will be ready for serving.

10-12 SERVINGS

NOTE This is often served with Arabic Bread (see page 12).

CHEESE PASTE
Labni

½ gallon plain yogurt
1 T. salt

Thoroughly stir the salt into the yogurt. Pour the yogurt into a cheesecloth bag (double thickness). Tie the top of the bag in a knot and hang it on the kitchen faucet. Drain overnight. When the yogurt becomes firm, remove it from the bag, place it in a bowl, cover, and refrigerate. Ultimately, it should be the consistency of softened cream cheese.

8 SERVINGS

CHEESE FILLED OMELET
Ijji bil-Labni

3 eggs
3 T. milk
salt and pepper to taste
2 T. butter
2 T. yogurt (see page 173)

Thoroughly beat the eggs with the milk and seasonings. Melt the butter in a frying pan. Pour the egg mixture into the pan and cook like an omelet; the bottom should be golden and the top barely cooked. Lower the heat and spread 2 tablespoons of yogurt on the center of the omelet. Carefully fold the omelet in half and cook another minute.

4 SERVINGS

NOTE In the Middle East, goat's yogurt is a special delicacy. Substitute goat's yogurt if desired.

PRESERVED YOGURT
CHEESE BALLS

Labni Makbusi

1 Yogurt recipe (see page 173)
olive oil

Drain the yogurt until it's very dry or until it resembles cream cheese. Take a table-spoon of it and put it in the palm of your hand, forming it into a ball the size of a walnut. Repeat until the yogurt is gone. Place the balls on a plate or tray for several hours. Pack them in sterilized pickle jars and cover with olive oil. Secure the lid and refrigerate until time of serving. When serving, spoon a small amount of olive oil over the yogurt balls for easier spreading.

8 SERVINGS

NOTE This spreads well on Arabic Bread (see page 12) or toast.

176

CUCUMBER-YOGURT SALAD
Khyar bil-Laban

1 small clove garlic
1 t. salt
1 T. dry mint, or 3-4 fresh stems and leaves
1 quart plain yogurt
2 cucumbers

Mash the garlic with the salt and fresh mint (if using dry mint, add below) in a bowl. Add the yogurt, blending well. Peel and cut the cucumbers in half lengthwise, then slice them in thin half-rounds. Add the cucumbers and the dry mint to the yogurt mixture. Fold together gently.

4 SERVINGS

NOTE This is especially refreshing in the summer.

EGGS IN MINT YOGURT SAUCE
Laban bil-Bayd

1 clove garlic
1 T. dried mint, or 3-4 fresh stems of mint leaves, discard the stems
1 T. salt
1 T. butter
1 T. cornstarch
1 c. water
1 quart plain yogurt
6 eggs

Mash the garlic, mint, and salt together, then sauté in the butter. Set aside. Dissolve the cornstarch in the water. Pour in the yogurt and mix well. Place the mixture in a heavy pot on a medium flame and bring to a boil, stirring constantly.

Break the eggs by striking with a knife and dropping them quickly into the boiling yogurt. Cook for 3-5 minutes, then add the sautéed garlic mixture and continue cooking for 15-20 minutes, or until the eggs are hard-boiled.

4-6 SERVINGS

NOTE Serve with plain rice.

178

Lamb Supreme with Yogurt

Laban ʾUmmu

2 lbs. lamb shoulder, cut into 2-inch chunks
5-6 small whole onions
1 egg
1 quart plain yogurt
1⅓ c. water
2 cloves garlic, crushed
2 T. dried mint or 3 T. fresh mint, chopped
1 T. salt
2 T. butter

Barely cover the lamb with water and cook for 30 minutes. Add the onions and continue cooking until the meat is tender.

In a pan, mix the egg, yogurt, and water well. Stir constantly over a medium flame for about 30 minutes. Pour this mixture over the meat and broth and let it simmer, stirring occasionally. Mash the garlic, mint, and salt together. Sauté in butter. Add to the yogurt mixture and cook until it thickens like gravy.

6-8 SERVINGS

NOTE Serve over vermicelli rice.

STUFFED LAMB DELICACIES IN YOGURT SAUCE
Shishbarak

½ Arabic Bread recipe (see page 12)

<table>
<tr><td>

FILLING

¼ c. pine nuts

2 T. butter

1 lb. finely ground lean lamb

⅛ t. allspice

⅛ t. cinnamon

salt and pepper to taste

2 medium onions, finely chopped

</td><td>

SAUCE

1 clove garlic

1 T. dry mint or 2 T. fresh mint, finely chopped

1 T. salt

3 T. butter

1 egg

2 c. water

1½ quarts yogurt

</td></tr>
</table>

Sauté the pine nuts in the butter until golden brown. Add the meat and seasonings and sauté until the meat is just browned. Add the onions and sauté for 5 minutes.

Roll the dough until it's ¼-inch thick and cut it into 2-inch rounds. Place a teaspoon of filling in the center of each circle. Fold the circle in half and pinch the edges together. Wrap the ends of what is now a crescent shape around your forefinger and pinch the dough together. (This looks like a fireman's cap.) Leave these out to dry for about 20 minutes, or, preferably, place them in a buttered pan and bake at 350° for 5 minutes.

For the sauce, mash the garlic, mint, and salt together. Sauté in the butter. Let stand. Beat the egg well with a fork. Add the water and yogurt, and mix well. Place the yogurt mixture on a medium flame, stirring constantly for 20-25 minutes or until it's thick like cream. Carefully add the stuffed pastry and cook for 10 minutes, stirring twice to prevent sticking. Add the mint-garlic mixture and continue cooking for 5 minutes.

8 SERVINGS

Eggplant with Yogurt
Batinjan bil-Laban

1 large eggplant
½ c. olive oil
1 clove garlic
1-2 t. salt
1 quart plain yogurt

Peel and slice the eggplant in ½-inch slices. Soak in salt water for 30 minutes. (This will prevent the eggplant from turning dark and from absorbing any excess oil when frying.) Remove and drain the eggplant on paper towels. Fry in the oil until golden brown on both sides. Cool.

Mash the garlic and salt together. Add the yogurt, mixing well. To serve, place the cooled eggplant on a platter and pour enough yogurt sauce to cover. Or, the eggplant and yogurt can be served separately.

4-6 SERVINGS

GARBANZO BEANS
WITH ARABIC CROUTONS
Fatti bil-Hummus

2 15½-oz. cans garbanzo beans
1 large clove garlic
salt to taste
2 medium loaves of Arabic Bread (see page 12), toasted
1½ c. plain yogurt
⅓ c. butter, melted

Bring the garbanzo beans to a boil, using one can of the bean liquid. Mash the garlic and salt together in large bowl. Add the hot garbanzo beans and liquid, mixing thoroughly. Break the bread into 1½-inch pieces, and layer each piece with yogurt then the garbanzo mixture. Top with warm melted butter.

4-6 SERVINGS

NOTE Although this can be served anytime, it is a favorite for breakfast.

LAMB SHANKS WITH ARABIC CROUTONS
Fatti Mqadim al-Ghanam

6 lamb shanks
1 stick cinnamon
⅛ t. allspice
salt and pepper to taste, plus 1 t. salt
1 15-oz. can garbanzo beans, drained
1 large onion, quartered
1 large clove garlic
2 medium loaves of Arabic Bread (see page 12), toasted
2 c. plain yogurt
⅓ c. butter, melted

Place the lamb shanks in a deep pot. Cover thoroughly with cold water. Add the seasonings, cover, and cook over medium heat. Remove the fat curd. When the meat is barely tender (fork pierces meat), add the garbanzo beans and onions.

Mash the garlic and salt in a large bowl. Pour 2 cups of broth from the lamb shank over the garlic and salt, mixing well. Cut the bread into 1½-inch-thick pieces. Debone the meat. In a soup bowl, place 1 layer of meat, followed by a piece of bread, then yogurt. Top with melted butter. If more liquid is desired, add broth.

4-6 SERVINGS

SAUCES
الصلصات

TAHINI SAUCE
Taratur

PARSLEY IN TAHINI
SAUCE
Baqdunis bit-Tahini

GARLIC SAUCE
Tum biz-Zayt

YOGURT SAUCE
Salsat al-Laban

YOGURT SAUCE
WITH MINT
Laban bin-Naʿnaʿ

TAHINI **IS USED AS A BASE** for sauces in the Middle East and is made from sesame seed oil. *Tahini* can be purchased at many grocery stores. Upon opening, stir the tahini, as the oil is usually separated. *Tahini* keeps indefinitely without refrigeration.

HINTS

~ When making anything with *tahini*, always blend water with the *tahini* first, then add the lemon juice. This makes for a whiter sauce.

TAHINI SAUCE

Taratur

1 clove garlic
1 t. salt
½ c. *tahini*
½ c. water
½ c. lemon juice

Mash the garlic and salt together. Add the *tahini*, mixing well. The sauce will thicken. Gradually add the water, blending thoroughly. Then add the lemon juice. Blend well.

4-6 SERVINGS

NOTE This can be a thin or thick sauce, depending upon use and preference. Simply adjust with lemon juice and water. This can be used with vegetables or in combination with other recipes.

187

PARSLEY IN TAHINI SAUCE
Baqdunis bit-Tahini

1 clove garlic
1 t. salt
½ c. *tahini*
½ c. water
½ c. lemon juice
½ c. parsley, coarsely chopped

Mash the garlic and the salt together. Add the *tahini*, mixing thoroughly. The sauce will thicken as you stir. Gradually add the water, softening the mixture. Add the lemon juice, blending well. Gently stir in the parsley.

4-6 SERVINGS

NOTE This is especially good as an appetizer dip, or served with grilled fish.

188

GARLIC SAUCE
Tum biz-Zayt

3 cloves garlic, minced
½ c. olive oil
¼ c. lemon juice
salt to taste

Mix all of the ingredients well.

6-8 SERVINGS

NOTE This goes well with broiled or grilled chicken. When eating, the chicken is dipped in the sauce. Garlic Sauce can also be used to brush chicken while broiling or grilling—just thin with more lemon juice.

189

Yogurt Sauce
Salsat al-Laban

1 egg, or 1 T. cornstarch
1 quart yogurt
1⅓ c. water
2 t. salt

In a pan, beat the egg well with a fork. (If you're using cornstarch, first dissolve it in ½ cup of cold water before blending it with the yogurt.) Add the yogurt and water, blending thoroughly for at least 5 minutes.

Place the pan on a medium flame and stir constantly with a wooden spoon in one direction for 20 minutes or until the sauce comes to a boil. This mixture may curdle or scorch if not watched carefully. Add the salt and continue cooking for a few more minutes.

6 SERVINGS

190

NOTE This is usually served with *Kibbi bil-Laban* (Kibbi in Yogurt Sauce).

Yogurt Sauce with Mint
Laban bin-Na'na'

1 large clove garlic
3 T. fresh chopped mint or 1 T. crushed dried mint
salt to taste
¼ c. butter
1 egg or 1 T. cornstarch
1 quart yogurt
1⅓ c. water

Mash the garlic, mint, and salt together. Sauté in butter and set aside.

In a pan, beat the egg well with a fork. (If you're using cornstarch, first dissolve it in ½ cup of cold water before blending it with the yogurt.) Add the yogurt and water, blending thoroughly for at least 5 minutes. Place on a medium flame and stir constantly with a wooden spoon in one direction. After 10 minutes, add the mint mixture and continue stirring, in one direction only, for 10 minutes more.

6 SERVINGS

191

NOTE This is usually served with *Laban 'Ummu* (Lamb Supreme with Yogurt), *Shishbarak* (Stuffed Lamb Delicacies in Yogurt Sauce), and *Kusa bil-Laban* (Stuffed Zucchini in Yogurt).

CONDIMENTS

البهارات

CRUSHED GREEN OLIVES
Zaytun Marsus

SPICED OLIVES
Zaytun Msabbah

STUFFED EGGPLANTS PRESERVED IN OIL
Batinjan Makbus biz-Zayt

STUFFED EGGPLANTS PICKLED IN VINEGAR
Batinjan Makbus biI-Khall

GRILLED GARLIC
Turn Mishwi

PICKLED CAULIFLOWER
Kabis al-Qarnabit

PICKLED TURNIPS
Lifit Makbus

PRESERVING GRAPE
LEAVES
Waraq 'Arish Makbus

SHEETED DRIED
APRICOTS
Qamaradin

DRIED APRICOTS
Mish Mish

FIG CONSERVE
Tin M'aqqad

QUINCE PRESERVES
Mrabba as-Sfarjal

OLIVES AND OLIVE OIL ARE essential to the Middle Eastern diet. Olives are served for breakfast, lunch, dinner, *maza* (appetizers), or snacks. My fondest memory is of dipping hot Arabic Bread in the olive oil as it came off my grandparents' presses in Lebanon. Another favorite childhood activity was to roll *Qamaradin* (Sheeted Dried Apricots) and hide it in my pockets for those sweet stolen moments during class when, hopefully, no one was looking.

CRUSHED GREEN OLIVES
Zaytun Marsus

1 lb. fresh green olives
salt to taste, plus 3 T.
½ lemon, quartered
¼ c. vinegar
1 or 2 small sticks of hot pepper (according to individual taste)
1 t. *za'tar*, optional
¼ c. oil
2 c. water

Place the olives on a board and crack them with a hammer like with walnuts. (The object is to crack the olives so that they open on one or several sides.) Place the olives in a bowl with water to cover and soak at room temperature for 24 hours. Drain and salt well, turning them over 4-5 times for another 24 hours.

Pack the olives in a quart jar, adding all of the ingredients. Dissolve the 3 tablespoons of salt in the water and add to the quart, filling it to cover the olives. Close tightly. The olives will be ready in 2-3 weeks.

1 QUART

NOTE Additional aging increases flavor. If the olives aren't well salted, they will become soft. *Za'tar* is available in Middle Eastern specialty grocery stores.

SPICED OLIVES

Zaytun Msabbah

1 lb. fresh green olives
2 small sticks of hot pepper
3 T. salt
2 c. water

Soak the olives overnight in water. Drain. Place all of the ingredients in a jar and fill the jar with water to cover the olives. Seal the jar. The olives will be ready in about 5-6 months.

1 QUART

NOTE   To make *Zaytun Mjarrah* (Slashed Olive Preserves), cut 4-5 slits into the olives before placing them in jars. Otherwise, follow the same procedure as above.

196

STUFFED EGGPLANTS PRESERVED IN OIL
Batinjan Makbus biz-Zayt

FILLING

2 c. walnuts, finely chopped

2 small heads of garlic, finely ground

salt to taste

2-4 c. olive oil

1 dozen Japanese eggplants, 3-4 inches long

Thoroughly mix the ingredients for the filling and set aside.

Wash the eggplants, pull the leaves off, and cut the stems short. Place the eggplants in enough boiling water to cover, and cook for about 10-12 minutes until the eggplants are barely soft. Drain and cool. Cut one lengthwise slit in each eggplant, leaving ½ inch uncut at each end to form a pocket. Place the slit side down and let it stand for 4-6 hours (or overnight) to drain.

Fill the inside pocket of the eggplant with a tablespoon or more of the filling, pressing it inside. Arrange the eggplants compactly inside quart jars. Place a dish over the opening of each jar. Turn the jar upside down onto a plate and let drain overnight. Any excess liquid may need to be drained by tipping the neck of the jar.

The following day fill the jars with oil (be sure the entire eggplant is well covered). Tightly close the jars. The eggplants will be ready in two weeks. Cut in rounds and serve.

6 SERVINGS

NOTE This is especially good as an appetizer.

197

STUFFED EGGPLANTS PICKLED IN VINEGAR

Batinjan Makbus bil-Khall

FILLING

2 heads of garlic, finely chopped

½ c. parsley, finely chopped

salt to taste

1 dozen Japanese eggplants, 3-4 inches long

2 c. red vinegar

1 c. water

Thoroughly mix the ingredients for the filling and set aside.

Wash the eggplants, pull the leaves off, and cut the stems short. Place the eggplants in enough boiling water to cover, and cook for about 10-12 minutes until the eggplants are barely soft. Drain and cool. Cut one lengthwise slit in each eggplant, leaving ½ inch uncut at each end to form a pocket. Place the slit side down and let it stand for 4-6 hours (or overnight) to drain.

Fill the inside pocket of the eggplant with 1-2 teaspoons of the filling, pressing it inside. Arrange the eggplants compactly inside quart jars. Place a dish over the opening of each jar. Turn the jar upside down onto a plate and let drain overnight. Any excess liquid may need to be drained by tipping the neck of the jar.

The following day mix the vinegar and water together. Fill the jars with the brine mixture (be sure the entire eggplant is well covered). Tightly close the jars. The eggplants will be ready in two weeks. Cut in rounds and serve.

6 SERVINGS

GRILLED GARLIC
Turn Mishwi

1-2 heads garlic

Bury the garlic heads in a barbecue's hot ashes for 15-20 minutes. Shell and serve hot.

6-8 SERVINGS

NOTE This is a favorite among people in the plains and the mountains of Lebanon... and they never have any colds!

PICKLED CAULIFLOWER
Kabis al-Qarnabit

199

1 large cauliflower
1 c. water
2 c. red vinegar
2 t. salt
4-6 small beets, optional

Wash the cauliflower and separate it into florets. Mix the water, vinegar, and salt together. Pack the cauliflower into clean, sterilized jars. Cover with the brine solution. Add 1 beet to every jar, if desired, and allow to stand for a week before using.

4 SERVINGS

PICKLED TURNIPS
Lifit Makbus

1 bunch of young small beets
4 lbs. turnips, sliced or quartered
salt
1 c. water
2 c. red vinegar

Boil the beets until they're done, about 20-40 minutes. Peel and slice the beets. Wash and trim the turnips. If the turnips are small, make ¼-inch vertical slices half way through the turnip, or if not, quarter into wedges. Put the turnips into sterilized quart jars with 1 or 2 beets in each jar. Add 1 teaspoonful of salt to each jar. Mix the water and vinegar and fill each jar to cover the turnips and beets. Seal the jars. The turnips will be ready in 2-3 weeks.

10-12 SERVINGS

NOTE The beets may be eliminated and ½ cup of beet juice may be substituted for half of the water. The beets impart a lovely pink color to the pickled turnips.

PRESERVING GRAPE LEAVES
Waraq ʿArish Makbus

40-60 grape leaves

Carefully wipe the individual leaves on both sides with a clean towel. Make uniform stacks of leaves with the stem ends on top of each other. Stack from 40-60 leaves, so they may be rolled and placed upright in cooled, sterilized jars. Place as many rolls upright as possible to make a compact fit. Place a hot sterilized lid on top and seal.

Store in a cool dry place. After opening, contents may be kept refrigerated for 2-4 weeks.

Sheeted Dried Apricots
Qamaradin

2 lbs. fresh apricots
½ c. sugar, adjust to desired sweetness

Wash and pit the apricots. Place them in a blender with the sugar and blend. Pour onto lightly greased cookie sheets, ¼-½-inch thick, cover with cheesecloth, and place in the hot sun for a few days until dry. The apricots can also be dried in the oven at 250° for 2-3 hours. Cut and serve in strips.

2 POUNDS

NOTE Sheeted *qamaradin* may be stored in the refrigerator for a long period of time. In the Middle East, large strips, covered with water, are placed in a bowl overnight, then eaten with sugar for breakfast.

Dried Apricots
Mish Mish

1 lb. fresh apricots

Wash and pit the apricots. Flatten them on a cookie sheets and let them dry in the hot sun for a few days. Cover with cheesecloth to protect the apricots. Store in the refrigerator.

1 POUND

FIG CONSERVE
Tin M'aqqad

1 lb. dried figs
1½ c. sugar
1 t. lemon juice
¼ t. powdered *mistki*, mustica, or Arabic gum, optional
1 T. anise seed
1 c. walnuts, coarsely chopped
¼ c. sesame seed

Chop the figs and place them in a pot. Barely cover the figs with water and simmer, stirring occasionally, until soft. Add the sugar (adjust depending on sweetness of figs), lemon juice, *mistki*, and anise seed and continue simmering. (The mixture will be thick and lumpy.) Add the walnuts and sesame seeds. Stir for a minute. Remove from the heat and cool. Store in sterilized jar or container.

2 QUARTS

202

NOTE *Mistki* or Arabic gum is available in Middle Eastern specialty grocery stores.

QUINCE PRESERVES
Mrabba as-Sfarjal

6-7 c. quince fruit
1 package MCP pectin
5½ c. sugar
¼ c. lemon juice

Wash, peel, and slice the quince in small pieces. Cover two-thirds of the fruit with water and simmer for about 25-35 minutes in a covered pot until done. Cool.

For every 4½ cups of cooked fruit, add 1 package of pectin. Mix well and stir occasionally for 30 minutes. Place the fruit back on the stove and bring to a boil. Add the sugar. When it comes to a hard boil, boil for 3-5 minutes. Pour the preserves into sterilized jars, to within ½ inch of the top, and seal.

2 QUARTS

DESSERTS
AND
BEVERAGES

الحلويات و الشراب

ROLLED COOKIES
Qras bis-Samin

NUT FILLED PASTRY
Ma'mul

NUT MOONS
Sambusik

SUZETTES WITH FILLING
Qtayif

BISCOTTI
Qirshali

BUTTER COOKIES
Ghraybi

LEBANESE MACAROONS
Ma'karun Khishshab

RICOTTA CHEESE
DELIGHT
Knafi bij-Jibin

SHREDDED WHEAT
PASTRY
Burma

RICE PUDDING
Riz bil-Halib

POWDERED RICE
PUDDING
Mhallabiyyi

SPICED RICE PUDDING
Mighli

CARMELIZED CUSTARD
Crème Caramel

ICE CREAM
Buza

CAROB TAHINI DIP
Dibs bit-Tahini

WHOLE WHEAT
WITH CONDIMENTS
Qamhiyyi

REFRESHING
YOGURT DRINK
Laban bis-Sikkar

CHERRY DRINK
Sharbat

SPICED TEA WITH NUTS
Ainar

ARABIC COFFEE
Qahwi

BECAUSE TRADITIONAL MIDDLE EASTERN FOODS are rich, fruit, which is plentiful the year round, is generally served immediately after dinner. Dessert is served later in the evening with coffee either at the dinner table or in the living room.

Some desserts are typical for certain holidays or special occasions. *Mshabbak*, *'awwaymat*, *sambusik*, *qtayif*, *zlabyi* *ma'karun khishshab* are special Christmas delicacies; *qtayif* and *zlabyi* might be served in mid-morning or for breakfast. *'Awwaymat* is traditionally served for Epiphany. The well known *baqlawa*, as well as *ma'mul*, *ghraybi*, and *burma* are Easter specialties, but they are also served throughout the year. *Mighli*, which is made basically from powdered rice and all kinds of spices, is served by the parents and family to guests to celebrate a newborn baby. *Qamhiyyi*, which is made of whole wheat grains, is served with condiments when a baby gets his or her first tooth.

Lebanese customs traditionally dictate the appropriate occasion for these desserts, but they can be eaten anytime.

HINTS

~ To draw or clarify butter, bring the butter to a boil, skim the top and place the clear substance in a separate container. The skimmed top and residue may be used in making rice or other dishes.

~ Typical seasonings used in making desserts are turmeric, saffron, anise, and caraway seeds.

~ Rose water and orange blossom water are commonly used instead of vanilla.

~ When using syrup, pour cold syrup on warm desserts for best results.

BASIC SUGAR SYRUP
Itir

2 c. sugar
1 c. water
couple drops of fresh lemon juice
1 t. rose water

Combine the sugar, water, and lemon juice in a saucepan. Boil over medium heat for about 10 or 15 minutes or until slightly viscous (225°). Before removing from the heat, add the rose water and let it come to a boil. Remove from the flame and cool.

½ PINT

NOTE *Itir* gets its name from a rose geranium. A leaf is boiled in the syrup. Orange blossom flavoring can be substituted for the rose water.

207

LAYERED PASTRY
Baqlawa

2 c. medium chopped walnuts, or pistachio nuts
⅓ c. sugar
1 T. rose water
1 lb. filo dough
1 lb. clarified butter

1 Basic Sugar Syrup recipe (see page 207)

Combine the nuts, sugar, and rose water. Take 2 filo sheets and brush them lightly with the clarified butter. Place 3-5 tablespoons of the nut mixture along the wide edge of the filo. Roll, as for a jelly roll, and place close together on a buttered 10 x 14-inch baking sheet. Brush the tops with butter. Cut diagonally into 2-3-inch lengths.

Bake at 300° until golden brown. Remove from the oven. Spoon cold syrup over each piece until saturated. (This takes about 3 applications of syrup per piece.)
10 SERVINGS

208

NOTE For a variation, spread the filo dough on a buttered 10 x 14-inch baking sheet, brushing each layer with butter. Half way through the layering, spread the nut mixture in a ½-¾-inch layer. Continue layering the buttered filo on top. Cut in diamond shaped pieces. Bake at 300° for one hour or until golden brown. Then pour cold syrup over the *baqlawa*, making sure the dough is well saturated.

FRIED DOUGH
Zlabyi

2 c. flour

1 T. vegetable oil, plus ½ c.

½ t. salt

1 t. *mahlab*, finely ground, optional

1 package cake yeast dissolved in ½ c. warm water and 1 t. sugar

1 c. powdered or granulated sugar

Mix the flour, a tablespoon of oil, salt, and *mahlab* in a bowl. Add the dissolved yeast. Mix it together with your hands until the dough becomes smooth. Let the dough rise in a bowl covered with a towel in a warm place for one hour.

Roll the dough until it's ⅛-inch thick on a floured board. Cut the dough into strips, about 2 inches x 6 inches. Various shapes can be made from the strips, such as a bow, which can be made by pinching the center. Pour ½ cup of oil in a skillet and heat to 350°. Drop the strips into the hot oil and brown them on both sides. Drain on absorbent paper and sprinkle with powdered or granulated sugar while still warm. Serve hot or cold.

8-10 SERVINGS

209

NOTE To test the temperature of the oil, drop a small piece of dough in and if it sizzles and the dough turns brown, the oil is ready.

EPIPHANY SWEET

'Awwaymat

1 package cake yeast dissolved in ½ c. warm water and 1 t. sugar
½ t. salt
1½ c. water
3. c. flour
2 c. vegetable oil

1 Basic Sugar Syrup recipe (see page 207)

Add the dissolved yeast, salt, and water to the flour. Mix thoroughly until a smooth dough is formed. Let rise 2-3 hours or until the dough has doubled in size.

Pour the oil into a skillet and heat to 350°. Take the dough in your left hand and gently squeeze it up between your thumb and forefinger, forming small walnut-sized balls. Using a teaspoon, scoop the balls off your hand and drop them into what should be at least 4 inches of heated oil (350°). Fry until golden brown and remove with a slotted spoon. Drain the balls on absorbent paper. Dip the drained balls into cold syrup and place on a platter for serving.

10-12 SERVINGS

COLORED ROSETTES
Mshabbak

1 Epiphany Sweet recipe (see page 210)
food coloring
2 c. oil

1 Basic Sugar Syrup recipe (see page 207)

Follow the basic recipe for Epiphany Sweet to make the dough. After the dough has risen, divide the batter into the number of different colors desired, then mix in the food coloring. Heat the oil in a skillet to 350°. Place the dough in a pastry bag with a $\frac{1}{8}$-$\frac{1}{4}$-inch opening and slowly squeeze the dough in a thin stream into the hot oil, forming 4-inch lacy rosettes. (This is formed by making the outside circle first and then filling in the center with an intertwined design.)

Fry until golden brown. Remove with a slotted spoon and drain on paper towels. Dip into the cold syrup with a slotted spoon. Place on platters for serving.

10-12 SERVINGS

Farina Squares

Nammura

2 T. *tahini*
4⅔ c. of farina
2½ c. sugar
1 c. clarifed butter
2⅓ c. milk
2 t. baking powder
1 T. vegetable oil
1 T. rose water
blanched almonds or pine nuts

1½ Basic Sugar Syrup recipe (see page 207)

Grease 2 8-inch square pans with *tahini* (sesame seed oil). Thoroughly mix the rest of the ingredients, excluding the blanched almonds or pine nuts. Pour the mixture into the pans. Place the whole blanched almonds or pine nuts on the top so that when cut into 1½-inch squares an almond or pine nut will be on each square.

Bake at 350° until golden brown, approximately 30-45 minutes. Check frequently so that it will not get too brown. Cut into squares, like brownies. Spoon cold syrup over the hot squares until all of the syrup is used.

24 SERVINGS

NOTE Cream of Wheat (28-oz. package), regular, may be substituted for the farina.

A CAKE DELIGHT
Sfuf

5 c. flour
1 T. baking powder
¼ t. saffron
1½ c. olive oil
2½ c. sugar
1 T. anise seed, powdered
blanched almonds

Sift the flour, baking powder, and saffron. Place in a large bowl. Add the oil and rub the mixture well between your palms until flaky. Add the sugar and anise seed; work it between your palms until it's thoroughly mixed. Add enough water to make it slightly softer than pie dough.

Spread the dough gently and evenly in an oiled 9 x 12-inch pan. Cut half way through the dough in 2-inch diamond shapes. Place a blanched almond on each diamond. Bake at 375° for 25-30 minutes. Then lower the heat to 200° and bake until golden brown. Test for doneness with a toothpick. When serving, cut through on the diagonal lines.

24 SERVINGS

213

LEBANESE CAKE WITH A FRENCH FLAIR

Gateaux

5 eggs
2 c. sugar
1 c. shortening
1½ t. vanilla
1¾ c. milk
3 c. flour
1 t. nutmeg
1½ T. baking powder
½ c. chopped nuts
½ c. chopped raisins

Separate the eggs. Beat the yolks until light lemon colored. Reserve the whites. Cream the sugar and shortening together until light and fluffy. Add the beaten egg yolks, vanilla, and milk. Mix. Sift the dry ingredients together and blend thoroughly into the sugar mixture. Beat the egg whites until soft peaks are formed. Fold the egg whites into the mixture followed by the nuts and raisins. Pour the batter into a greased angel food pan. Bake at 350° for 1 hour or until a toothpick comes out clean.

16 SERVINGS

LEBANESE CAKE DOUGHNUTS
Ka'k

3 eggs
peel of 1 lemon, grated
2⅔ c. sugar
1 c. clarified butter
1 c. yogurt
7 c. flour
1 t. baking soda

Beat the eggs with the grated lemon peel until light and fluffy. Add the sugar, butter, and yogurt. With the palm of your hand blend the ingredients together pressing against the bottom of the bowl until the sugar no longer has texture. Then gradually add the flour and baking soda to the egg mixture. Continue mixing by hand until the dough is thoroughly blended. (A small additional amount of flour may be needed for ease in handling the dough.)

Take a walnut-sized piece of dough and roll it into a log ½ inch x 6 inches—or the desired length. Shape in a circle, overlap the ends, and pinch together. Place on a barely oiled baking sheet. Bake at 350° until they are golden brown on the top and bottom.

7-8 DOZEN

NOTE Sugar, butter, and yogurt may be blended with the eggs with a mixer for a crisp cookie.

DATE CRESCENTS
Qras bil-ʿAjwi

FILLING

3 c. dates, ground

2 T. butter

½-1 c. walnuts, optional

½ t. powdered *mistki* (pound *mistki* seed with mortar and pestle), optional

metal clamps used for decorating cookies ~ *malqat*

2 c. clarified butter, congealed

¾ c. sugar

½ t. *mahlab*, finely ground, optional

6 c. flour

½ package cake yeast dissolved in ¼ c. warm water

¾ c. lukewarm milk

Combine the filling ingredients, mix well. Set aside.

Cream the butter, sugar, and *mahlab* by mixer at medium speed. Add the flour and dissolved yeast and complete the mixing by hand. Gradually add the milk, kneading to a soft dough. Let the dough rest for 1 hour.

Roll the dough into sheets of ¼-inch thickness and cut out into 2-inch rounds. Place a spoonful of filling on half of the round. Fold the top half over, sealing the edges together to make a half moon-shaped cookie. Pinch and seal the edge of each cookie. Prick a design on top with a fork or a *malqat* (a metal clamp used for decorating cookies). Bake at 350° for 20-25 minutes until light golden.

7-8 DOZEN

NOTE If a *malqat* is not available, use *tabiʿ* or leave the cookies plain. *Malqat* is used only on flour dough; *tabiʿ* may be used on either flour or farina dough. These cookies may be kept for 2 weeks in an air-tight container.

ROLLED COOKIES
Qras bis-Samin

5 c. flour
$\frac{1}{2}$ t. *mahlab*, finely ground
$1\frac{1}{2}$ c. sugar
$\frac{1}{2}$ t. salt
$\frac{1}{2}$ t. cloves
$\frac{1}{2}$ t. allspice
$\frac{2}{3}$ c. shortening
$\frac{2}{3}$ c. clarified butter, at room temperature
$\frac{1}{2}$ package cake yeast, dissolved in $\frac{1}{4}$ c. warm water
$\frac{1}{2}$ c. milk

Mix all of the dry ingredients. Add the shortening and rub the dough between your hands; add the butter and continue rubbing.

Make an indentation in the middle of the flour mixture. Add the dissolved yeast and milk. Start mixing and kneading thoroughly from the center. (The dough should be soft like pie dough.) Cover and set aside for 45 minutes.

Roll the dough into 3-inch rounds about $\frac{1}{4}$-inch thick. Flute the edge and prick a design on top with a fork or a *malqat* (see page 216); or use a cookie cutter. Place the rounds on an ungreased cookie sheet. Cover with a cloth and let stand for 30 minutes. Bake at 350° until golden brown. Let stand until cold. Pack and freeze if desired.

7-8 DOZEN

NOTE If desired, brush the tops of the cookies with beaten egg yolks for a glaze, just before baking.

Nut Filled Pastry
Ma'mul

FILLING

3 c. ground walnuts, almonds or pistachios

1 c. sugar

1 T. rose water

2 c. clarified butter, congealed

½ c. sugar

6 c. flour

1 c. lukewarm milk

½ c. powdered sugar

Thoroughly mix the filling ingredients with a spoon and set aside.

Cream the butter and sugar until light. Add the flour, working with your hands until the dough is well blended. Gradually add the milk, kneading to a soft dough. Place a walnut-sized chunk of dough in the palm of your hand. Using your forefinger, press and expand the hole in the center of the dough by rotating and pressing the dough against the palm of your hand until the shell is ¼-inch thick and about 3 inches long. Place a teaspoonful of filling into the shell. Carefully close, forming a sphere. (Other shapes can be formed or use a *tabi*'—a wooden cookie mold.)

Place the spheres on an ungreased baking sheet and bake at 350° for approximately 20-25 minutes, until the bottoms are light brown. Sift powdered sugar over the cookies while still warm. Let them stand on the baking sheet until completely cooled. Remove.

6-7 DOZEN

NOTE Date filling may be substituted, see page 216. These cookies may be kept for 2 weeks in an air-tight container if placed in a cool place.

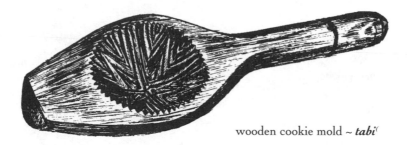

wooden cookie mold ~ *tabi*

VARIATION

2 c. clarified butter, room temperature
6 c. farina or Cream of Wheat
2 T. flour
1 c. warm milk

Melt the butter. Thoroughly mix the butter with the farina. Cover and let stand overnight or let stand a minimum of four hours. Add the flour and slowly add the warm milk. Knead the dough thoroughly until it's soft and can be easily shaped by hand. Use this in *Ma'mul* and other nut or date filled sweets instead of a flour-based dough.

NUT MOONS

Sambusik

2 c. clarified butter, congealed
½ c. sugar
1 t. *mahlab*, finely ground, optional
6 c. flour
⅔ c. milk or water

FILLING

3 c. walnuts, ground
1 c. sugar
1 T. rose water

½ c. powdered sugar

Cream the butter, sugar, and *mahlab* until light. Add the flour, milk or water and knead by hand until smooth. Roll the dough until it's ¼-inch thick then cut with a 2-inch round cookie cutter. Combine the filling ingredients. Place one heaping teaspoon of filling on each round. Fold and close the open edge by pinching with your fingers or a fork. Shape into half moons. Lay each cookie on an ungreased baking sheet about ¼ inch apart. Bake at 350° for 20-25 minutes until light brown. Sift powdered sugar over the top while they're still hot.

7-8 DOZEN

Suzettes with Filling
Qtayif

2 c. flour
2 eggs
2 T. shortening
½ c. sugar
1 t. salt
1 package cake yeast dissolved in ¼ c. warm water
1¼ c. water

FILLING
1 lb. ricotta cheese
1 c. sugar

1 c. clarified butter
1 Basic Sugar Syrup recipe (see page 207)

221

Combine all of the suzette ingredients and blend well. Cover and let rise for 2 hours. Combine the filling ingredients. Pour 4-inch pancakes on a buttered medium-heated pancake iron or frying pan. Cook until the tops are bubbly. Do not turn over. Place one heaping teaspoon of filling on top of each pancake. Fold in half and press the edges closed. Arrange on a well-greased baking sheet and brush the tops generously with the butter. Bake at 400° for about 15 minutes. Spoon syrup, 2 or 3 times, over each suzette, depending on desired sweetness. May be served hot or cold.

10-12 SERVINGS

NOTE This is popular for special breakfasts. To make the suzettes with a walnut filling, mix 1 cup ground walnuts, ½ cup sugar, and 1 teaspoon rose water.

BISCOTTI

Qirshali

5 c. flour
1 T. baking powder
1 c. oil
5 eggs
1¼ c. sugar
1 t. vanilla
1 T. anise seed
½ c. white raisins, optional
2 egg yolks, slightly beaten

Sift the flour and baking powder together, add the oil and rub the mixture together with your hands. Beat the eggs and sugar together, then add the vanilla and anise seed. Pour the egg mixture into the flour mixture and work together with your hands. Mix in the raisins. The dough mixture will be sticky. Let it rest for several minutes. Spread the dough into 2 slightly greased 9 x 12-inch pans (the dough should be ½-inch thick). Brush the tops with the egg yolks. Bake 30 minutes at 350°.

Take the biscotti out of the oven and cut them into ½ x 3-inch fingers. Place them on their sides leaving space between the cookies. Some will need to be transferred into a second pan. Return to the oven, lower the heat to 300°, and cook for 20 minutes more until slightly brown. When done, these cookies will be crisp.

4-5 DOZEN

BUTTER COOKIES
Ghraybi

1 c. clarified butter, congealed
1 c. sugar
½ c. flour
1 c. blanched almonds or pine nuts

Thoroughly cream the butter. Add the sugar and continue creaming with a mixer until fluffy (5-10 minutes). Add the flour and work the dough with your hands until smooth. If it's too sticky, add a little more flour. Shape the dough into either an S-shape or ½-inch-thick rounds. Press the center of the round with your thumb and place a blanched almond or pine nut in the center.

Place the cookies on an ungreased baking sheet. Bake in the oven at 300° for 13-15 minutes. The cookies should be very pale in color. Let them stand for 6 hours or until completely cooled as they are very flaky and will easily fall apart when warm.

2-3 DOZEN

223

LEBANESE MACAROONS
Ma'karun Khishshab

5 c. flour
1 T. baking powder
1½ c. olive oil
1½ c. sugar
1 T. anise seed

2 Basic Sugar Syrup recipes (see page 207)

Sift the flour and baking powder together in a large bowl. Add the oil and rub the dough well between your palms until flaky. Add the sugar and anise seed and continue to work the dough between your palms until it is thoroughly mixed. Add enough water to make it slightly softer than pie dough.

Take a handful of dough and roll it into a ½-inch rope on a slightly floured pastry cloth. Cut into 3-4-inch strips. Gently roll each strip over a solid surface that has a design (such as a colander, sieve, or grater). The cookies will have a pressed design on one side and finger imprints on the other.

Place the cookies on an ungreased baking sheet with the pressed design upward. Bake at 375° for 15-20 minutes until a light golden brown.

Remove from cookies from the baking sheet and while the cookies are still warm, dip each cookie in cold syrup. If all the cookies are not to be used immediately, they can be stored and dipped into hot syrup just before serving. The cookies can be eaten without syrup if desired.

5-6 DOZEN

NOTE Two teaspoons of rose water may be substituted for the anise seed.

RICOTTA CHEESE DELIGHT
Knafi bij-Jibin

2 lbs. ricotta cheese
1 c. sugar
1 lb. *burma* (or *knafi*) dough (see page 226)
1 c. clarified butter

1 Basic Sugar Syrup recipe (see page 207)

Combine the cheese and sugar. Place half of the *burma* dough on a generously buttered 10 x 14-inch baking sheet, and gently press the dough over the bottom of the
pan. Brush the top with butter. Spread the cheese mixture on top of the dough and
top with the remainder of the dough, spreading evenly and gently. Brush the top
generously with butter. Bake at 300° for 1 hour or until golden brown. Remove
from the oven and while hot, pour the cold syrup over the top. Serve in squares, hot
or cold.

16 SERVINGS

225

SHREDDED WHEAT PASTRY
Burma

3 c. chopped walnuts, pistachio, or hazel nuts
¾ c. sugar
1 T. rose water
1 lb. *burma* (or *knafi*) dough
1 c. clarified butter

1 Basic Sugar Syrup recipe (see page 207)

Combine the nuts, sugar, and rose water. Place half of the *burma* dough on a generously buttered 10 x 14-inch pan, gently pressing the dough over the bottom of the pan. Brush the top with butter. Spread the nut mixture on top of the dough. Evenly place the remaining dough on top of the nut mixture. Brush generously with butter. Bake at 300° for 1 hour or until golden brown. Remove from the oven. While hot, pour cold syrup on the *burma*. Cut into squares. Serve cold.

16 SERVINGS

NOTE *Burma* literally means round. In the Middle East, it is made into snail and jelly roll shapes by working the *burma* dough on a large, well-buttered sheet forming a flat compact layer that can be filled and rolled. If *burma* or *knafi* dough is unavailable, shredded wheat cereal may be substituted. Slightly crush and layer the cereal instead of the *burma* dough in a well-buttered pan, then it's ready to use.

Regular shredded wheat biscuits may be individually stuffed with the filling by hollowing a pocket with a knife. Place the biscuits on a well-buttered cookie sheet. Brush them generously with butter. Bake at 300° for 25-30 minutes. While hot, pour cold syrup on the biscuits. Serve cold.

RICE PUDDING
Riz bil-Halib

1 c. white rice
3½ c. water
3 c. milk
1½ c. sugar (adjust to desired sweetness)
1 T. rose water

Wash the rice well, drain, and place in a pot. Add the water, cover, and simmer over a medium flame for 15-20 minutes. Add the milk, stirring constantly. When it begins to thicken, add the sugar and rose water. Continue stirring constantly until the rice is soft or well done. (When it is the consistency of a cream filling.) Remove from the flame and pour the mixture onto a platter, spreading thinly. Cool and serve alone or with fruit.

6-8 SERVINGS

227

POWDERED RICE PUDDING
Mhallabiyyi

1 c. powdered rice
4 c. water
3 c. milk
1½ c. sugar
1 T. rose or orange blossom water

Combine the powdered rice, water, and milk. Cook over a medium flame, stirring constantly until the mixture starts to thicken. Add the sugar, lower the heat, and simmer until thick or until it's the consistency of a cream filling, approximately 30 minutes. Add the rose water, bring it to a fast boil, and remove immediately. Pour onto a platter or into individual bowls. This may be eaten warm or cold but is most commonly eaten cold.

6-8 SERVINGS

SPICED RICE PUDDING
Mighli

1 c. powdered rice
2 c. sugar
7 c. cold water
1 t. caraway seed
1 t. anise seed or 2 T. *bharat* (mixture of spices especially for *mighli*)
½ t. cinnamon
½ t. ginger
¼ c. pine nuts, blanched almonds, and chopped walnuts

Combine all of the ingredients, with the exception of the nuts. Cook over a medium flame, stirring constantly until the mixture starts to thicken or is the consistency of a cream filling, about 30-35 minutes. Pour into bowls. Chill and garnish with the nut mixture before serving.

6-8 SERVINGS

229

NOTE Coconut may be substituted for the nuts. *Bharat* is available in Middle Eastern specialty stores.

CARMELIZED CUSTARD
Crème Caramel

½ c. sugar, plus 4 T.
4 eggs
1 t. vanilla
2 c. milk

Carmelize the sugar by placing it in a cast iron skillet over moderate heat and stir constantly until the sugar is melted. When the sugar is the desired tawny color, pour it into a baking dish and quickly coat the sides and bottom with the melted sugar.

Beat the eggs well with the vanilla. Mix the milk with the remaining 4 tablespoons of sugar and add it to the eggs. Pour this mixture over the solidified sugar in a 5-cup baking dish and place the dish in a pan of hot water.

Bake at 350° until a knife inserted into the custard comes out clean (approximately 45 minutes). Cool. When unmolded, the melted caramel runs down the sides forming a sauce.

6 SERVINGS

ICE CREAM

Buza

4 c. milk
3 T. corn starch or *sahlab*
1¼ c. sugar
⅛ t. ground *mistki*

Scald the milk and remove it from the heat. Dissolve the corn starch in a little cold water and add it to the milk. Return the milk to the heat, stirring constantly until it boils, then add the sugar. Cook until slightly thickened. Add the ground *mistki*, stirring continuously. Cool. Pour the mixture into an ice cream maker and freeze according to the manufacturer's instructions.

4 SERVINGS

NOTE *Mistki* or Arabic gum is available in Middle Eastern specialty grocery stores.

231

CAROB TAHINI DIP
Dibs bit-Tahini

1 c. *dibs* (carob syrup)
¼ c. *tahini*
1 loaf Arabic Bread (see page 12)

Mix the *dibs* and *tahini* until well blended. Dip the bread into the mixture and eat by hand.

10-12 SERVINGS

NOTE Unsalted crackers may be substituted for bread. This is usually served at breakfast, but may be eaten at other times.

232

Whole Wheat
with Condiments
Qamḥiyyi

2 c. whole wheat kernels
¼ t. salt

CONDIMENTS
sugar
walnuts, coarsely chopped
raisins, white preferable
rose water, in a droper

Place the well-rinsed, whole wheat kernels and salt in a pot and cover generously with water. Bring to a full boil, reduce the heat, and cook until tender, about 30-45 minutes. Add additional water if necessary to keep the kernels well covered.

To serve, put the condiments in individual bowls. Place the cooked wheat kernels and liquid in a large dish. Serve individually with the desired condiments, adding only 1 or 2 drops of rose water. (Too much rose water will leave a bitter taste.)

8-10 SERVINGS

NOTE In Lebanon, this is often served to guests in celebration of a baby's first tooth.

REFRESHING YOGURT DRINK
Laban bid-Sikkar

1 c. yogurt
½ c. water
1-2 t. sugar (adjust to taste)

Place all of the ingredients in a blender and blend on high speed for a few seconds. If a thicker or thinner consistency is desired, adjust the proportion of yogurt and water. Serve in a tall drinking glass.

1-2 SERVINGS

NOTE This is extremely refreshing in the summer. Strawberries, blackberries, and other fruits may be included.

CHERRY DRINK
Sharbat

1 lb. red cherries
1 c. sugar
1-2 T. Basic Sugar Syrup (see page 207)

Wash, drain, and pit the cherries. Alternate layers of cherries with ¼-inch layers of sugar in an enamel, glass, or stainless steel pan. Let stand 5-6 hours until the sugar has completely drawn the juice from the cherries. Drain the liquid into a pan and bring to a full rolling boil. Store in the refrigerator. This syrup will keep up to 6 months.

To serve, place 1-2 tablespoons of the syrup in a tall glass of water with ice.

1 PINT

Spiced Tea with Nuts

Ainar

1 T. caraway, powder
1 T. cinnamon
1 T. anise seeds
⅛ t. nutmeg
4-5 c. water
sugar to taste
pine nuts, walnuts, and blanched almonds

Boil the spices in the water for 5 to 7 minutes. Strain through a fine sieve or gauze. Into each prepared tea cup place 1 or 2 tablespoons of nuts and sugar to taste; fill the cup with the hot spiced water.

4 SERVINGS

NOTE This is traditionally served when a baby is born and is always served with a teaspoon. Coconut may be added in addition to the nuts.

235

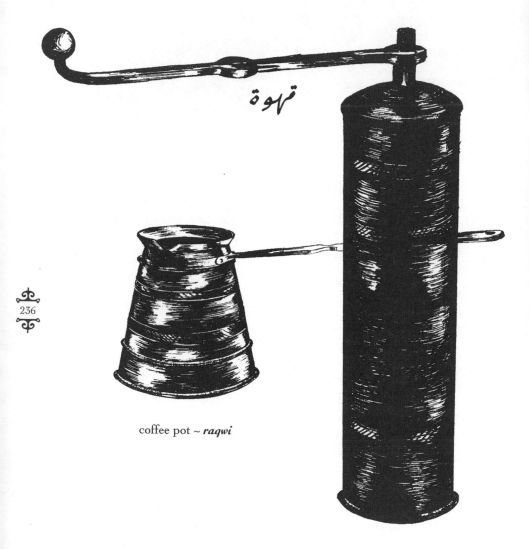

قهوة

coffee pot ~ *raqwi*

coffee grinder ~ *tahuni*

ARABIC COFFEE
Qahwi

Arabic coffee is often referred to as "Turkish style coffee" and is not only a treat but an honor bestowed on the guest by the hostess. Two basic pieces of equipment are required: the small *raqwi* or coffee pot (a small sauce pan would work too) and a *tahuni* or coffee grinder. Coffee beans are ground fresh at every serving and coffee is made in small quantities, from 2 to 6 demitasse cups. The finely ground coffee available at many coffee shops also works.

Arabic coffee is usually served at the end of the meal and when there is company. The coffee is served black and bitter during sad occasions, and sweet during weddings or happy occasions. Most of the time it is served *mazbut* or "just right."

Measure and pour 1 demitasse cup of cold water per person into the *raqwi*. For each cup add 1 heaping teaspoon of finely powdered coffee and 1 teaspoon of sugar (depending on desired sweetness). Place on a medium flame and stir until the ingredients are well mixed. Bring to full rolling boil. As it boils up, foam is formed and a little froth is spooned into each demitasse cup.

Some households prefer letting the coffee come to a boil 3 times. After each boil, remove the pot from the heat until the foam recedes. Spoon a little froth into each cup. Repeat the process 2 more times.

NOTE Arabic coffee may also have exotic flavoring: either 1 cardamom pod (for 3-4 demitasse cups) is placed in the coffee when it is boiling, or a little urn of rose water is passed around for a drop in the cup.

SUGGESTED MENUS

1. LENTEN (MEATLESS)

Cauliflower with Taratur *Qarnabit bit-Tahini*
Grilled Fish *Samak Mishwi*
Lebanese Bread Salad *Fattush*
Fresh Fruit
Turkish Coffee

Pickled Turnips *Lifit Makbus*
Fish with Rice *Sayyadiyyi*
Green Bean Salad *Lubyi Mtabbli*
Arabic Bread
Spiced Rice Pudding *Mighli*
Turkish Coffee

Triangle Meat Pie *Ftayir*
Fava Bean Patties *Falafel*
Eggplants with Yogurt *Batinjan bit-Laban*
Vegetable Salad *Slatat al-Khudar*
Colored Rosettes *Mshabbak*
Turkish Coffee

Crushed Green Olives *Zaytun Marsus*
Fried Vegetables *Khudar Miqliyyi*
Lentil Pottage *Mjadra*
Purslane Salad *Slatat al-Farfhin*
Arabic Bread
Whole Wheat with Condiments *Qamhiyyi*
Turkish Coffee

Eggplant Salad *Batinjan Mtabbal*
Baked Fish with Tahini Sauce
      Samak bit-Taratur
Potatoes with Taratur Sauce
      Batata bit-Tahini
A Cake Delight *Sfuf*
Turkish Coffee

II. Meat

Stuffed Zucchini *Kusa Mihshi*
Stuffed Grape Leaves
   Mihshi Waraq 'Inab
Vegetable Salad *Slatat al-Khudar*
Suzettes with Filling *Qtayif*
Turkish Coffee

Tabbuli
Baked Chicken *Djaj Mishwi*
Garlic Sauce *Tum biz-Zayt*
Farina Squares *Nammura*
Turkish Coffee

Spiced Olives *Zaytun Msabbah*
Baked Chicken *Djaj Mihshi*
Baked Kibbi *Kibbi bis-Sayniyyi*
Cucumber-Yogurt Salad *Khyar bil-Laban*
Turkish Coffee

Stuffed Tripe and Casing Supreme
   Ghammi
Grilled Kibbi *Kibbi Mishwiyyi*
Tomato Salad *Slatat al-Banadura*
Fresh Fruit
Turkish Coffee

Triangle Meat Pie *Ftayir*
Baked Kafta *Kafta bis-Sayniyyi*
Green Bean Salad *Lubyi Mtabbli*
Rice Pudding *Riz bil-Halib*
Turkish Coffee

III. Special Occasions

'Arak
Meat Rolls Supreme *Sambusik bil-Lahm*
Chicken with Vegetables par Excellence
   Mlukhiyyi
Arabic Plain Rice *Riz Mfalfal*
Nut-Filled Pastries *Ma'mul*
Turkish Coffee

Stuffed Eggplants Preserved in Oil
   Batinjan Makbus biz-Zayt
Garbanzo Bean Dip *Hummus bit-Tahini*
Grilled Kafta *Kafta Mishwiyyi*
Grilled Meat Kabobs *Lahm Mishwi*
Tabbuli
Arabic Bread
Assorted Sweets *Mihli*
Turkish Coffee

'Arak
Brain Appetizer *Nkha'at Mtabbli*
Supreme Lamb Stew with Kibbi
   Kibbi Qarnabiyyi
Triangle Meat Pie *Lahm bil-'Ajin*
Arabic Bread
Powdered Rice Pudding *Mhallabiyyi*
Fresh Fruit
Turkish Coffee

241

GLOSSARY OF ARABIC TERMS

This glossary includes the Arabic words for ingredients and utensils used in making the recipes. The colloquial rather than the classical Arabic is used. The final *t* and *yyi* are dropped, as these endings are usually dependent on words that follow or precede them. (See introduction for pronunciation.)

Adas lentils

ʿAjin dough

ʿAjwi dates

ʿArabi Arabic

ʿAraq anise flavored alcoholic beverage made from grapes; the national drink

ʾArdishawki artichoke

ʿArish *see* **Waraq**

ʾArnab rabbit

Bamyi okra

Banadura tomatoes

Baqdunis parsley

Baqlawa many-layered pastry

Baqli purslane

Batata potatoes

Batinjan eggplants

Bazilla peas

Bayd eggs

Bharat a blend of seasonings

Bizzaq snails

Burghul crushed wheat; usually comes in fine (#1), medium (#2), and coarse (#3). Cracked wheat or bulgur wheat is not a satisfactory substitute

Burma dough that resembles shredded wheat; also referred to as **Knafi** dough

Dibs carob syrup

Dilᶜ ribs from meat or leafy vegetables

Daj chicken

Farfhin purslane; *see* **Baqli**

Fasulya lima beans

Ful fava beans

Furn term used for Arabic bread made commercially

Habash turkey

Halib milk

Halyun asparagus

Hashwi stuffing

Hindbi dandelion greens

Hummus garbanzo beans or chick peas

Hwahis giblet

Ijji omelet

ᶜIqdi Safra saffron

ᶜItir syrup made with rose geranium leaves. Orange or rose water essences are often substituted.

Kabis pickled, preserved; *see* **Makbus**

Kafta finely ground lean meat

Kaᶜk hard rolls or small cakes, similar to doughnuts

Khall vinegar

Khubz bread

Khudar vegetables, greens

Khyar cucumbers

Kibbi ground meat with *burghul*

Kishi *laban* and *burghul* fermented together, dried and ground

Kizbara coriander

Kmaj round, flat bread with pocket used for sandwiches, dips, Arabic pizzas, etc.

Knafi *see* **Burma**

Kusa summer squash

Laban yogurt or cultured milk

Labni yogurt cheese paste made from dehydrated *laban*

Lahm meat

Laqtin a vegetable similar to pumpkin

Laymun Bus Sfayr a fruit found in hot climates; flavor can be simulated by combining one part grapefruit juice and two parts lemon juice

Lifit turnips

Lsanat tongues

Lubyil green beans

Lubyi Msallat black-eyed peas

Mahlab a seasoning used in dough or pastries. *Mahlab* is a small seed of the stone of a wild cherry, used originally in perfumes and medicines

Maᶜkaruni refers to pastas (spaghetti and macaroni)

Makbus pickled, preserved (in vinegar or oil)

Malfuf cabbage

243

Malqat metal clamp used in decorating (by pinching) cookies

Marquq very thin, round, flat bread, rolled like Italian pizza dough

Maza appetizers or hors d'oeuvres

Mazahir orange blossom essence

Maward rose water

Mawzat meat shanks

Mdaqa large wooden mallet

Mihli assorted sweets made with filo dough

Mihshi stuffed meats or vegetables

Miqli fried

Mish Mish apricots

Mishwi grilled

Mistki Arabic gum, commonly referred to as *mustica*

Mlabbas sugar-coated almonds

Mlukhiyyi green leafy vegetable, known also as "Jew's mallow"

Mnazli stew; refers to dishes made with eggplants or other vegetables as the basic ingredient

Mcianiq sausage

Mrabba jam

Na'na' mint

Nayyi raw

Nkhi'at brains, lamb or beef

Qarnabit cauliflower

Qasbi liver

Qdami roasted and unsalted garbanzo beans

Raqwi Arabic coffee pot

Rawbi a starter or culture for making yogurt

Ris rice

Sahlab extracted from tubers of any of various orchids and used like tapioca; corn starch may be substituted

Saj paper-thin bread that is baked over a metal dome on an open fire

Salso sauce

Samak fish

Samni the Middle East equivalent of butter

Sanamura herring

Sayniyyi pan

Sbanikh spinach

Sfarjal quince

Sharbat beverages

Sh'iriyyi vermicelli

Shurba soup

Sikkar sugar

Silq Swiss chard

Simmaq tart, ground seasoning from seed of sumac tree

Siyami Lenten

Slata salad

Smid grain similar to regular Cream of Wheat, semolina, or farina; used for cake and filled-cookie dough

Tabi' wooden cookie mold

Tahini heavy sesame seed oil (not the type used in Oriental cooking)

Tahuni coffee grinder

Taratur *tahini* sauce

Tin figs

Tlami round, flat, soft-textured bread without pocket used for *mnaqish* and as regular bread

Tum garlic

Waraq leaves used in *mihshi*; such as grape, Swiss chard, and cabbage

Waraq 'Inab or **'Arish** grape leaves

Waraq Malfuf cabbage leaves

Waraq Silo Swiss chard leaves

Yakhni stew; refers to dishes made with potatoes as the main ingredient

Zafra meat curds appearing when cooking meat in water

Za'tar plant found in the Middle East; also refers to a seasoning blended from *za'tar*, thyme, marjoram, *simmaq*, and salt

Zankha a special "meaty" smell or feel associated with uncooked meat

Zayt oil

Zaytun olives

INDEX

247

249

250

255